Be Your Own Boss

Matt Avery

For UK order enquiries: please contact Bookpoint Ltd,
130 Milton Park, Abingdon, Oxon OX14 4SB.
Telephone: +44 (0) 1235 827720. Fax: +44 (0) 1235 400454.
Lines are open 09.00–17.00, Monday to Saturday, with a 24-hour
message answering service. Details about our titles and how to
order are available at www.teachyourself.com

Long renowned as the authoritative source for self-guided learning –
with more than 50 million copies sold worldwide – the **Teach Yourself**
series includes over 500 titles in the fields of languages, crafts, hobbies,
business, computing and education.

British Library Cataloguing in Publication Data: a catalogue record
for this title is available from the British Library.

This edition published 2010.

The **Teach Yourself** name is a registered trade mark of
Hodder Headline.

Typeset by MPS Limited, A Macmillan Company.

Printed in Great Britain for Hodder Education, an Hachette
UK Company, 338 Euston Road, London NW1 3BH, by
CPI Cox & Wyman, Reading, Berkshire RG1 8EX.

The publisher has used its best endeavours to ensure that the URLs
for external websites referred to in this book are correct and active
at the time of going to press. However, the publisher and the
author have no responsibility for the websites and can make no
guarantee that a site will remain live or that the content will remain
relevant, decent or appropriate.

Hachette UK's policy is to use papers that are natural, renewable
and recyclable products and made from wood grown in sustainable
forests. The logging and manufacturing processes are expected to
conform to the environmental regulations of the country of origin.

Impression number   10 9 8 7 6 5 4 3 2 1
Year   2014 2013 2012 2011 2010

Front cover: Photo Alto/Photolibrary.com

Back cover: © Jakub Semeniuk/iStockphoto.com, © Royalty-
Free/Corbis, © agencyby/iStockphoto.com, © Andy Cook/
iStockphoto.com, © Christopher Ewing/iStockphoto.com,
© zebicho – Fotolia.com, © Geoffrey Holman/iStockphoto.com,
© Photodisc/Getty Images, © James C. Pruitt/iStockphoto.com,
© Mohamed Saber – Fotolia.com

Contents

Meet the author

After years of working for big corporations and becoming increasingly frustrated by having to dance to someone else's tune I finally decided to take the leap to becoming my own boss and set up my first company, a marketing consultancy, in 1997. I loved it from the very first day, and despite experiencing a good many pitfalls and pratfalls along the way I have never stopped loving it! With the benefit of hindsight, I realized I had been woefully unprepared for the realities of being my own boss, but having been bitten by the bug of being answerable only to myself (not to mention keeping all the rewards of my hard work) I launched my second company, a copywriting agency, in 2001. This time I was able to draw on my experiences, detailed in this book (along with the experiences of many other soloists), and things went a lot more smoothly. In both cases there were significant challenges, of course, but with them came significant opportunities, often ones which I hadn't even begun to imagine. Someone once told me that the worst day of being your own boss still beats almost every day you spend with someone else as your boss and I have to say I agree. And after so many years of working for myself, do I have any regrets? Just one. Like so many people who take the leap to becoming their own boss my only regret is that I didn't do it sooner!

Matt Avery

Only got a minute?

Becoming your own boss is one of the most exhilarating – and daunting – things you can ever do in your work life. So how can you ensure you maximize the benefits while minimizing the risks before, during and after taking the leap?

Leaving your job in the best way possible can provide invaluable help, particularly in the early days of running your business, and establishing and maintaining a database of useful contacts will not only provide practical assistance but will also deliver a readymade support network to provide a much needed boost when the going gets tough.

You will also need to establish a clear vision for your business, create a workable business plan and roadmap with realistic targets and problem-solving strategies, and decide how you are going to measure its progress over the next year, three years, five years etc. You will need to create a robust framework for maximizing the potential of your business and achieving the optimum work/ life balance, including deciding on such factors as whether or not you should rent an office space (private or shared) or perhaps work from home, and how best to combine your work life with your home life. Learning how best to motivate yourself in the short, medium and long term will be crucial to your success as a soloist and it's important to remember too that while being your own boss can be hard work you should also learn how to enjoy its many benefits, not least the flexibility your new working life affords you.

As you become more established in your solo work life, you will need to concentrate on developing and growing your business, learning how to leverage the advantages of being your own boss, and how to identify and negotiate the myriad potential pitfalls. What are the best practices for dealing with clients? How should you structure and manage your finances? How will you avoid becoming isolated while at the same time ensuring family and friends do not encroach on your work time and space? How can you grow your business through the employment of mobile technologies? And for those times when the going gets tough you will need to have strategies in place to inspire you and to ensure you keep moving your business forward, in the desired way and at the required rate.

So whether you have decided to become your own boss to escape the rat race and keep all the rewards of your hard work, whether redundancy has forced you to rethink your options but also provided you with the opportunity to do something new and exciting, or whether early retirement has afforded

you the chance to start the career of which you
always dreamed, now is your chance to maximize
your work/life potential.

How will you get the very most out of being
your own boss?

5 Only got five minutes?

Have you ever wondered what it would be like to be your own boss, to be answerable to no one but yourself and to keep all the rewards of your hard work? Are you excited by the possibilities of running your own business and managing your career, but daunted by the realities and practicalities of working for yourself? Is it time you took the leap to becoming your own boss?

For some people the motivation to such a career step-change is the opportunity to escape the rat race and shape their work life to accommodate their needs and desires, implementing a long-held dream and keeping all the rewards of their hard work; for others, the need to rethink their options is unexpected and perhaps unwanted, forced upon them through redundancy or the need to take early retirement, but they are determined to seize this sudden opportunity to do something new and exciting and implement a completely new career; and some people just want to do something completely different, to shake up their routine and start afresh in their work life, to stop living at work and start working and living by taking charge of their own destiny and managing their career the way they want to. And of course the end goal will be different for everyone who takes the brave leap to becoming their own boss too – some people want to build an empire, while others want to remain working for and by themselves; some people dream of making millions, while others dream of achieving the perfect work/life balance (even if it means taking a pay cut). Whatever your reasons for wanting to become your own boss and whatever your ambitions for your new business and lifestyle, being fully prepared to negotiate the potential pitfalls and pratfalls of solo working will enable you to get the most out of your new career and capitalize on the opportunities with which you are presented.

When you are considering going solo, there are four key areas you need to anticipate in order to implement a successful transition to working for yourself:

- ▶ consider whether you are really suited to being your own boss
- ▶ find out how to set up your new working life to the best advantage
- ▶ learn how to develop your business and maximize its potential
- ▶ be prepared to manage the practical aspects of working for yourself.

Practical exercises are an invaluable way to help you to determine the best course of action for you at each stage of your new business life, while real-life examples from people all around the world who have successfully become their own boss will inspire you and give you food for thought.

Before embarking on this career step-change for yourself you will need to think about the following questions:

- ▶ Do you have what it takes to become your own boss? Is it really the best course of action for you?
- ▶ How will you quit your job to best effect, so that it provides you with a springboard to your new working life?
- ▶ Do you understand what being your own boss actually means? Have you thought about how best to set up your solo working life, including how to make the most of working from home and how to balance your home life with your work life?
- ▶ Have you considered how you will accentuate the positives of being your own boss, leveraging its advantages and minimizing its disadvantages?
- ▶ Do you understand the different ways in which you can enjoy your new-found freedom and flexibility and how to capitalize on these to help make your business more successful?
- ▶ Do you know how to motivate yourself when the going gets tough and how to set realistic targets for your business?
- ▶ Will you be able to combat the loneliness of the solo worker?
- ▶ Do you know how to create business plans and roadmaps to successfully grow your business as a soloist?
- ▶ Do you know any problem-solving strategies to combat some of the most common difficulties faced by soloists?
- ▶ Are you able to deal with clients to best effect?

- Do you know how to manage all the practical aspects of being your own boss, from getting the financial aspects right to setting up the perfect IT infrastructure for your business?
- Can you maximize your effectiveness in managing all aspects of your business?

By studying real-life case studies of people who have made the leap and succeeded you can gain invaluable lessons and insight into how to successfully move your own business forward (often against the odds), as well as the reassurance that no matter what obstacles you may be faced with and no matter how insurmountable they may seem you are not alone – everyone who takes the brave decision to become their own boss faces myriad difficulties along the way.

Motivation will be key, in the short, medium and long term, and through the application of a variety of motivational techniques you can learn how to maximize your potential, both through rewarding yourself for success and spurring yourself on through the thought of failure and what that would mean for your business and your work life. You also need to learn how to look after yourself as a solo worker – how to avoid feeling isolated, to keep energized and mentally stimulated, and to keep physically fit and active now that you no longer have a commute or an office complex, factory floor, school building etc. to negotiate in your day-to-day working life.

If you like the idea of becoming your own boss but you are not sure that it would suit you or that you would suit it, you may like to start by taking baby steps. By becoming a '5-to-9er', working evenings and weekends on your new business so that you can test your offer in the marketplace, you can also see if you enjoy the lifestyle of working for yourself before you commit to doing so full time.

Whatever your aspirations for your business and for your work life, being fully prepared to be your own boss will enable you to make the most of the opportunities which are presented to you, and to create opportunities where there are none, while negotiating any potential roadblocks and hazards.

Foreword

Anyone can start up a business. You don't need experience or lots of cash, just imagination, courage and a good dose of determination. At least that's where it all began for me.

I was working in a 'normal' job, getting a bit bored with the same-old, same-old when I decided to take the plunge and set-up on my own. I didn't have any wealthy relatives or financial reserves on the side. It was just me, a small loan and a grant from the Prince's Trust. But the one thing I had – and still have to this day – is a heartfelt passion for what I do.

Henry Ford once summed up the way I feel about life rather succinctly. He said: 'If you think you can, or think you can't, you're right.' Everyone has within them what it takes to succeed, there's no doubt about that. You just need to dream big. And my dreams certainly know no boundaries.

Starting a business is hard work but it is extremely fulfilling. If setting-up on your own is your dream, go for it. Don't hold back and end up as the person who nearly did something great. Be the person who wanted success and grabbed it with both hands. That's what I did anyway!

Secret Millionaire Liz Jackson MBE, CEO of Great Guns Marketing

Member of the Board of Companions of the CMI

Introduction

'It is not because things are difficult that we do not dare,
but it is because we do not dare that things are difficult.'

(Seneca, Roman philosopher)

Have you ever caught yourself dreaming of escaping the never-ending rat race? Of leaving behind the myriad niggles and drawbacks of working for someone else, of ditching the commute and the office politics and breaking out on your own, doing things your way? Have you ever imagined what it would be like to be answerable to no one but yourself, to dictate your own destiny and to keep all the rewards of your hard work?

Have you ever dreamt of becoming your own boss?

If you have you are far from alone. Self-employment, once seen as the preserve of the brave few, is now truly mainstream. According to smarter working campaign Work Wise UK more than 3.4 million UK workers have already taken the plunge and quit their jobs to work for themselves – that's more than 12 per cent of the total workforce. The Bureau of Labor Statistics reports that in the US the figure is 25 million. In Asia it is nearer 60 million and globally there is reckoned to be a staggering 150 million people who have taken the leap to becoming their own boss.

What's more, that number is steadily on the increase. According to a recent report published by National Savings and Investments, 20 per cent of Britons would like to leave behind the drudgery of the 9-to-5 working life to run their own business.

Yet research suggests that quitting your job and going solo is perilously difficult. According to the US government, an alarming 95 per cent of all small businesses fail within the first five years. In the UK, an average of 471 businesses go bust every week, according to a report by Industry Watch. But why?

The answer is simple. Among the many possible reasons and explanations there are two reasons that account for the vast majority of new business failures:

▶ *a failure to understand the realities and requirements of becoming your own boss*
▶ *inadequate planning and preparation.*

It sounds simple enough, but if it were then 95 per cent of all new businesses would succeed, not fail. The harsh reality is that the vast majority of people who quit their job to become their own boss find the transition fraught with unseen pitfalls and dangers, and they quickly see their dream turning into a nightmare because they just can't work out how to make their new working life work for them – and to be frank it is hardly surprising.

Whether the leap of faith to becoming your own boss means leaving the security of a large company to branch out on your own in a familiar field, or whether you are setting up your own small company from scratch in a completely new business area (perhaps to fulfil a dream of turning a passion or hobby into a full-time job), becoming a self-reliant and self-sufficient solo worker is one of the most liberating, daunting, rewarding, terrifying, exhilarating 'What-the-hell-have-I-just-done?!' moments in your entire life. And while the actions required and the consequences experienced will vary according to your particular field of work and the business model you select for yourself, there are also a great many elements which are common to everyone when they become their own boss – not least among them that the transition is undeniably life-changing. So how do you ensure the change is positive?

'Forewarned is forearmed'

While there are no quick solutions to guarantee a seamless – and painless – transition, by understanding the realities of what awaits you and the major differences between being in someone else's employ and being your own boss you can prepare yourself, your environment, your family, your business network etc. to make the change as smooth as possible. And once you are firmly ensconced in your new way of life, understanding the pitfalls and pratfalls of solo working – and how to avoid them – is half the battle. The other is turning every difference to your advantage, accentuating every positive (and potential positive), and creating positives where there simply aren't any and quite possibly where they don't even belong. This book shows you how.

Be Your Own Boss provides practical advice through an exploration of solo working gained from case studies and interviews with a plethora of people who have been there, done it, and been successful – although in most cases the transition was far from smooth. It provides genuine, tried-and-tested tips and practices which *really work*, with pen portraits of solo workers from across the globe covering careers as diverse as wedding photography, marketing consultancy, film making, oven cleaning and aviation services, to name but a few. Equally diverse were the set-ups and business ambitions of people becoming their own boss, with some people happy to earn the same as or even less than they were whilst in paid employment but who wanted more free time to spend with their families and enjoy their hobbies, while others had a clear vision to have made £1 million-plus within the first five years of running their own company. Some people had made the leap to becoming their own boss by quitting a good job in a company they liked, some had left a job they hated just as soon as they were able; others seized an unexpected opportunity presented by redundancy, while some had opted to begin a second career after they had taken early retirement. Some made the leap to becoming their own boss straight away while others built up their business in their evenings and weekends before leaving their job to concentrate on their business full time. For some people the biggest joy would be to work on their own, while others were determined to build a sizeable staff for their company as quickly as possible.

Each one's story is different, each person's journey unique. Yet there is a huge amount of common ground in their journeys to working for themselves with a great many rules of thumb and strategies relevant to everyone who wants to make a success of becoming their own boss.

This book will take you step by step through all the necessary processes, and guide you in your decision making as you benefit from their collective experience, creating the book each said they wished they had been able to read before embarking on their own life-changing career move!

> **'People know you for what you've done, not for what you plan to do.'**
>
> (author unknown)

So, if you are determined and ready to take the leap to becoming your own boss, dive straight into this book at Chapter 4, 'Quitting your job' (unless you're reading this book because you've already done so, in which case feel free to skip ahead to Chapter 5, 'What becoming your own boss actually means – and how to do it'). If on the other hand you are as yet undecided whether or not to leave your job, and if you do so whether or not to become your own boss, the next two chapters will help you to make an informed decision.

Acknowledgements

The author gratefully acknowledges the invaluable input provided by the many people from all over the world (including Argentina, Australia, Canada, France, Germany, Holland, Singapore, South Africa, the UK and the USA to name but 10!) who so generously gave their time, knowledge and the fruits of their experiences to provide insight, inspiration and a plethora of top tips for being your own boss. In particular I would like to express my sincere gratitude to Anne, Brian, Carmen, Clare, Claudia, Dave, Diego, Estevan, Gaynor, Greg, Ian, Jake, Jamie, Sylvia and Vijay. Thanks too to all my family and friends for their continued encouragement and support. And special thanks to my creative partner, David, for his help, expertise and very special brand of humour in the face of adversity!

Dedication

To Suze, for her tireless support and undimmable enthusiasm.

1

Weighing the options

In this chapter you will learn:
- *whether you should stay put or it is time to leave*
- *whether you can improve your situation without leaving*
- *the pros and cons of quitting and of becoming your own boss*

Should you stay put or is it time to leave?

> '**Whenever you see a successful business, someone once made a courageous decision.**'
>
> Peter Drucker

The lure of becoming your own boss can be incredibly strong, particularly if things are not that great in your current job or if you have a burning desire to take charge of your own career destiny. The opportunity to work for yourself and to be answerable to no one but yourself, whilst keeping all the rewards of your efforts, can certainly seem mightily attractive. But it is important to keep a sense of perspective and to remember that there can be significant downsides to going solo too. Before taking the leap to solo working, therefore, you will need to be very clear about your reasons for doing so. Have you reached the end of the road in your current job? Are you bored, and craving a new challenge? Have you really fully explored all the other options open to you (a sideways move within the same company, taking a similar job within a different company, changing careers altogether but remaining in salaried employment etc.) or have you been blinded by the thought of being your own boss? Have you thought through the practicalities of leaving? Have you given yourself sufficient time and space to really understand what it is you want from your new career? Have you achieved everything you wanted to achieve whilst in paid employment? Will you be missing out on valuable training and experience by leaving? It is only through a process of rigorous self-examination and soul-searching, as well as an exploration of all the options available to you, that you can reach a considered opinion as to which direction to take in the next step along your career path.

Case study

'Having achieved the goals I had set myself in my old company (to become MD), I began looking around for the next goal. I gradually realized that I did not want any of the jobs the people "above" me had, they were all political, inward-looking roles. It also dawned on me that now that I was the boss I had no one to look up to and learn from, other than the corporate suits, and I did not want to learn about global business management, P&L reporting or sitting in endless internal meetings discussing company finances. I also looked at my remuneration package and found that despite the fact that I was solely responsible for 30 per cent of the 100-person company's revenues, I was still paid a standard salary and that even with the best bonus the company had ever paid anyone (which they begrudgingly paid me) I was never going to make serious money – the kind of money that the firm's founders had made when they sold the company (and my career) to a big corporation. All this led me, with much soul-searching (was I being too greedy? was I too selfish? shouldn't I be grateful?), to hand in my resignation. I had to do it several times over six months as it was not accepted and pushed back with offers of more money, a better title (really) and "we need to think about it", before I finally arranged to meet the top boss for breakfast out of the office with a typed signed letter in my hand. Job done.'

Not only do you need to be clear as to your reasons for leaving, but you need to be clear about what you will be taking on. It is important to fully understand the realities of becoming your own boss and to take the time to appreciate what you will be leaving behind if you do decide to go solo as well as to understand the challenges with which you will be faced. The grass, as they say, is always greener on the other side. A considered approach at this stage, weighing up your options and thinking through the consequences of your actions should you decide to take the leap to becoming your own boss can save you a lot of time, heartache and money further down the line. If becoming your own boss is not the right career move for you, or not at this time, then it is best to be honest with yourself and find out now. If it is, going into it with your eyes open and your expectations realistic will help you to derive maximum benefit from your new career right from day one.

Case study

'I chose to leave my previous employer once I had achieved my main goals with them. I had reached the age when the pension was payable (i.e. outside of the pension trap) and I had gained training, a range of sought-after skills, qualifications and experience that made me marketable and attractive as a consultant. I was lucky because the Royal Navy have a very good and comprehensive resettlement package. This provides some general resettlement courses, but I focused some weeks of training on "Small Business" and "Managing a Successful Business" courses. These ensured I started my business correctly and eased my way into profit.'

First things first – working for other people is not a bad thing *per se*, nor is self-employment necessarily a good thing, and becoming your own boss is certainly not for everyone; it all depends what you are looking for. For many people, working in a normal, paid job is just fine and it does have some undeniable advantages. It is predictable (which makes it feel stable), the income is guaranteed, paid holidays are included and the work finds you, not the other way around; for many self-employed people the constant drudge of trying to find the next piece of work or the next profitable workstream is one of the biggest drawbacks to becoming their own boss – and for many employed people the safety and security afforded by having a steady job where finding the work is someone else's responsibility outweighs not owning the company or getting to keep all the profits. Paid employment also usually involves working in a shared space, be it an office, a warehouse, a factory or wherever, which means you have company and a social element to your working life – something which is absent from the day-to-day working lives of most people who have decided to become their own boss as this usually means working on their own, at least to begin with. Being employed offers a secure and predictable structure to your working life and to your opportunities for promotion and salary advancement, as well as a ready-made support network – and so on and so on. So while there are a great many fantastic advantages to becoming your own boss there are also some significant plus points to being in someone else's employ. It is therefore vital that you have weighed up all your options, and fully understood all the pros and cons of being in someone else's employ versus being self-employed before you actually take the leap and begin the transition to becoming your own boss – a transition which can be long, complicated and very hard work.

Q: What were the most daunting/difficult elements of the change to becoming your own boss?

A: Having to deal with the small things ... from finding the right accountant, to fixing IT issues, from buying the right PC to finding support. I was used to focusing on my work and on my clients' needs ... all of a sudden I had to deal with practical matters ... I am not very good at that! The most challenging was finding the right help and support ... I made a few mistakes.

Can you improve your situation without leaving?

If you are unsure as to whether or not you wish to take the leap to becoming your own boss, one of the first things you will need to do is to determine whether it is likely, or even possible, that those elements of your work life which dissatisfy you can be changed; and if they can be how long will it take to change them? Equally, you need to decide whether or not those things which you would love to see in your work life are realistic and, if so, how long they would take to implement. The following exercise will help you to draw a clear picture of your situation.

First, make a list of the major bugbears in your working life, those things you feel would need to change in order to tempt you to remain in your current employment. Try to limit your list to a maximum of about ten items (if you find that this is not nearly enough then you probably do not need the rest of the exercise to tell you that it is time to move on!). Now draw a simple two-axes graph on which to plot the points you have identified. On the X axis chart the degree of difficulty (time and/or effort required) of achieving each of your aims. On the Y axis rate the level of importance, so that something that you feel is crucial but difficult or slow to implement will be in the top right corner and something that is less important and easier/quicker to implement will be in the lower left corner.

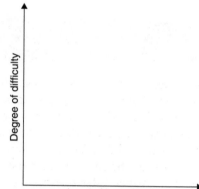

Next make a list of all those things which would be introduced into your work life, not in an ideal world, but in a better *yet still realistic* world. Again, try to limit your list to a maximum of about ten items. Draw another chart identical to the one you have just completed and plot the points accordingly.

Now draw a vertical line down the middle of both charts and ignore everything on the left hand side. If they are not sufficiently important to you to have made it into the right-hand side then they really should not influence your 'Should I stay or should I go?' decision. Of the remaining points on each chart, how many are in the top half and how many in the bottom half? What is the percentage difference between the two? If the vast majority in chart 1 are in the top right-hand corner, then most of the aspects which are really important to you and would need to be improved to make your current working life tenable are very unlikely to be achieved any time soon, if at all, and even if they are the process is likely to be drawn-out and painful. Likewise, if the majority in chart 2 are in the top right-hand corner then most of the new elements you would like to see introduced to give you the working life you desire are very unlikely to happen, at least any time soon. So if the majority of the points you have identified as needing to change, improve or be introduced are in the top right portion of your charts, it may well be time to move on.

Case study

'You have two choices in life – to live your own life and reach your own potential or to contribute to someone else's dreams and help realize theirs. I am not being pejorative here – for some people a life's work is about helping someone else's cause that they feel a connection with. So be careful to make your choice – this is the easiest time in history that anyone has been able to express themselves and realize their own dreams – so make an informed choice.'

If you feel that moving on is the best option for you then the next decision is whether you opt to move to a similar company and work in a similar field or use this useful re-evaluation of your situation as the spur to move on to something completely new. This will depend on a great many factors, but whatever you decide you will be taking positive action to rectify a poor situation and that, surely, can only be a good thing. On the other hand, if most of the points are in the bottom right-hand corner then the things that matter to you most are reasonably easy to alter, perhaps even speedily, and staying put but with a better working situation and maybe an improved deal might be your best option. If this is the case then you will want to gather the low-hanging fruit first, so start working your way through the list from the lower right-hand corner (the most important and easiest to achieve) to the top left-hand corner (the least important and most difficult to achieve). This way you will begin to improve your situation to the maximum degree in the shortest possible time.

Pros and cons of quitting and of becoming your own boss

Prior to taking the leap to becoming your own boss it is important to understand the pros and cons involved. These will, of course, vary from person to person since different aspects of quitting your job and becoming your own boss will assume varying degrees of importance to each individual. Indeed, some aspects which might be a positive change for one person might well be a negative change for another person, and vice versa, such as working alone all day. A good way to understand the implications to you and your future business is to compile two lists, one documenting the upsides of quitting your job and becoming your own boss and the other documenting the downsides.

> **Insight**
>
> The pros and cons of leaving salaried employment to become your own boss are inherently personal and may even be diametric opposites from one person to the next, so try not to be influenced too much by other people's opinions and recommendations. Remember that one man's meat is another man's poison ...

It is imperative that you compile your lists as accurately as possible, charting those factors which you predict will have a major bearing on your decision, so take your time to ensure your lists are as comprehensive as possible. You might like to use the following lists as a starting point, but they must not be considered exhaustive since such lists can never be all things to all people. Instead, use them as a starting point to give you some food for thought, adding anything which you feel is relevant and deleting any points which you feel do not really relate to you. You might even wish to swap some of the remarks in each list from one column to the other!

Pros of quitting your job and becoming your own boss
- *leaving behind all the office politics*
- *doing away with the commute*
- *working to your own timeframe*
- *working when and where best suits you*
- *personal self-growth*
- *spiritual self-growth*
- *emotional self-growth*
- *self-empowerment*
- *no more worrying what the parent company would think of XYZ*
- *no more endless calls on your time to no value*
- *being tangibly rewarded for hard work and success*
- *no more inflexible work structures*
- *achieving a better work/life balance*
- *freedom*
- *being answerable and accountable only to yourself*
- *keeping all the rewards of your efforts*
- *the feeling that everything is possible and that it is up to you*
- *the opportunity to pursue more creative and imaginative work interests*
- *the opportunity to work in a broader field*
- *new challenges*
- *being able to see more of your family*
- *an increase in quality time when and where it counts.*

Cons of quitting your job and becoming your own boss
- *no more guaranteed salary*
- *no more admin support*
- *loss of a circle of colleagues who offer support*
- *it is cold outside – forget the rose-tinted spectacles, it can be very lonely and very hard work*
- *no one to rely on, nobody else to blame*
- *fear of the unknown*
- *marching headlong out of your comfort zone*
- *being faced with a blank canvas where it is up to you (and destiny) to paint the picture – and your future*
- *isolation*

- *loneliness*
- *loss of IT infrastructure/support*
- *financial insecurity*
- *loss of a pre-defined work/life structure*
- *loss of external input/influence*
- *risk.*

Once you have completed your lists you will need to assign a value to each of your points, 10 meaning that it is crucially important to you and 1 meaning that it has little or no importance. Take your time over this because it is really important to determine exactly what is important to you in your working life and in achieving an optimal work/life balance in order to make an informed decision as to your future career path. Then reorder your lists with the most important at the top and the least important at the bottom. Now get rid of everything with a value of five or less. What you are left with are those factors which are *really important to you*, the ones you should use in helping to determine whether or not taking the leap of faith to becoming your own boss is worth the risk and all the hard work it will entail. It will also give you a clearer idea of the framework you use to identify what you need/desire from your work life.

Case study

'At the time I considered working for another company. I think that a part of me wanted a sense of security and a feeling of belonging to something bigger. After interviewing with a few companies nothing seemed right. Immediately after quitting I had a few projects commissioned, thus the transition was quite easy and smooth – natural. I grew up thinking that it was all about climbing the corporate ladder but circumstances changed my framework, my paradigm.'

If your lists suggest that the downsides to going solo outweigh the upsides then you will need to think long and hard about why you are drawn to becoming your own boss in the first place and whether your expectations of this lifestyle are realistic. If you still think that they are, then revisit the lists to see which of these factors you would be willing and able to re-prioritize. Be careful to be completely honest with yourself here though – it is far too easy to let a desire for a major shift in your work life blinker you to the realities of becoming your own boss, and ignoring the downsides now because you wish that they were not true or that they did not apply to you can prove to be a costly mistake.

Insight

If you feel you really would like to become your own boss but the tests are showing you that you are unsuited to the vagaries of this lifestyle, you may like to consider investing in some life coaching. A skilled life coach will help you to understand what it is you really need to change in your life and why you perceive becoming your own boss as the answer.

If your lists suggest that the pros to becoming your own boss outweigh the cons for you, in all those areas where it matters most, then becoming your own boss might well suit you. Your next job is to determine whether or not you suit it.

KEY THINGS TO REMEMBER

▶ *Be clear about your reasons for wanting to leave your job and become your own boss.*

▶ *Determine whether or not it is possible to change your current job sufficiently to give you what you need in your working life.*

▶ *Identify the pros and cons of quitting your job together with the pros and cons of becoming your own boss.*

▶ *Decide which of those elements are absolutely crucial to you.*

▶ *If you are not 100 per cent certain that you want to take the leap to becoming your own boss (which is quite different from being ready to do so) you may wish to consider the benefits of investing in some life coaching to help you understand more about what you are really looking for from the move.*

▶ *Make sure you fully understand the realities of taking the leap to becoming your own boss before you commit to it.*

▶ *Think through all the drawbacks to becoming your own boss, as well as the advantages.*

▶ *Make sure you have a clear and realistic understanding of the downsides of leaving paid employment and the downsides of becoming your own boss, and ensure you are prepared to meet the challenges.*

▶ *Ensure you genuinely think the upsides to leaving paid employment and becoming your own boss outweigh the downsides – by a considerable margin.*

2

Are you cut out to be your
own boss?

In this chapter you will learn:
- *whether you have what it takes to go solo*
- *about yourself and who you think you are*
- *about psychometric profiling*
- *how to plan your future paths*

Do you think you have what it takes to go solo?

> **'Some people dream of success ... while others
> wake up and work hard at it.'**
>
> (author unknown)

You may have spent many hours dreaming of becoming your own
boss, and you may even be quite certain that the potential benefits
to be gained outweigh the risks involved. But do you have what it
takes to go solo? Are you the sort of person who will thrive working
on their own day in and day out, fighting to secure the necessary
work and managing your own time and your own abilities to
ensure your company remains solvent? Or will you soon tire of the
novelty of being your own boss once the cold hard reality sets in –
the realization that now you have gone solo the buck stops with
you and the support network on which you have come to depend
has now evaporated? Do you have the personality, approach and
outlook to thrive working on your own? The move to becoming

your own boss can certainly be exhilarating and liberating, but it can also be daunting and even terrifying in equal measure. You will almost certainly feel a sense of isolation and loneliness on occasions, and this will only exacerbate any doubts you may have that you did the right thing in leaving your erstwhile employer to become your own boss. And just when you are feeling exposed and vulnerable, the nagging doubts that you may not succeed, that you are not sure how you are going to make ends meet this month, that this was all a horrible mistake, will rear their ugly heads to taunt you.

Insight

In thinking through whether or not to become your own boss, make sure you are absolutely clear as to whether you are in it for the short, medium or long term as this will colour your judgement in a great many ways.

So, before severing the umbilical cord of paid employment and making the leap to becoming your own boss you need to ensure that you are the sort of person who will thrive under such sometimes adverse conditions. You may like to gather the opinions of family and friends who know you well as to whether they think you would sink or swim as your own boss, but remember that they may only tell you what they think you want to hear, for fear of hurting you. In addition, then, you will need to engage in some rigorous soul-searching and the first step is to determine your personality profile.

Who do you think you are?

It is far too easy to perceive yourself as the sort of person you wish to be, and it is true that the majority of us paint a somewhat different picture of ourselves in our heads than the one which most accurately represents us. So, much as we might like to be the ideal candidate to go solo and become our own boss, it is imperative before making such a radical change to our working and indeed our personal life that we are as certain as we can be that we really do have the right sort of personality to make a success of it.

Of course we can never be completely certain, and some people who would appear to be naturals for becoming their own boss make the leap only to find that they have made a horrible mistake and quickly turn back to the safety of regular employment, while others who would not seem to be cut out for becoming their own boss thrive and quickly build a successful and profitable company. In doing everything we can to determine whether or not we are likely to succeed, however, we are starting off on the right foot and giving ourselves every chance to succeed. So how can you find out if you have the right personality type to become your own boss?

Insight

The real question is not 'Where do you want to be in one year/five years/ten years?' nor even 'What do you want to be?' The real question is 'Who do you want to be?'

The good news is that you can be pretty sure that you do not have completely the wrong personality type to successfully become your own boss! Consider this: if you were 100 per cent happy in your current employment you would not be reading this book. The same applies if you know 100 per cent that you would hate to become your own boss or that there is simply no way you could make it work for you. So it stands to reason that with considering the change – a big change – to solo working you are looking for a change not only in your working life but in your life in general, and a pretty major change at that. Which is good, because that is exactly what the transition to becoming your own boss offers you. It was interesting to note the most frequently used words and phrases when asking respondents to describe how their move to becoming their own boss had changed them:

- ► *happier*
- ► *healthier*
- ► *nicer to know*
- ► *friendlier*
- ► *more relaxed*
- ► *liberated*
- ► *more in control*
- ► *wiser.*

As you can see, it was their attitudes towards not just their work but their lives in general, and even how it had changed them as a person, which were the most prominent factors. This is part of the opportunity that the move to becoming your own boss affords you. However – and it is a big 'however' – the respondents were all people who had made a successful transition to self-employment. In many cases it had been a struggle and rarely had it been plain sailing all the way, but they had got there in the end, and successfully. They had what it takes. Knowing whether or not you do is fundamental to understanding whether you are likely to make a success of it and the first step is understanding what your key personality traits are, both in and out of the workplace:

▶ *What assets or hindrances might you bring to the transition and to your new career?*
▶ *What support might you need along the way?*
▶ *What changes might you need to make to your current lifestyle?*
▶ *What additions to your skill set may be required?*
▶ *What might you need to work on, or at least keep an eye on, with regards your personality?*

The best way to understand all the relevant elements of your personality and how they correspond to the workplace, and how you can use the insight this gives you to help inform your decision with regards your career path, is to take a psychometric profiling test.

Psychometric profiling

Psychometrics is the field of study concerned with determining an individual's primary personality traits through the theory and technique of psychological measurement. As such it can be a useful tool in helping to determine whether or not you have the right sort of personality as well as the necessary drive to become your own boss. In other words, if you think it might be right for you but you are not certain, you love the idea of it but you are not sure whether you would love it or hate it in reality, then a psychometric profiling study might help you to determine your best course of action. Attitude and aptitude are measured, qualified and quantified and respondents are typically assessed via the application of measurement instruments such as questionnaires and self-administered tests, so they are easy to complete in your own time whenever it suits you, although you will need the results to be professionally analysed. Be honest with your answers – an accurate psychometric profile will really help you to see if you are likely to find the transition from paid employment to becoming your own boss easy or difficult, or indeed nigh on impossible. If you are tempted to just give the answers you think you need to give in order for it to determine that you are perfectly suited to becoming your own boss, remember that a good psychometric test will often include questions the purpose of which is not immediately apparent. For example, 'If you receive an unexpected telephone call from the police would you immediately begin to feel guilty, worried or excited?' or 'Would you prefer an evening out with friends eating a meal in a restaurant or going with the same friends to a bowling alley?' Trying to 'cheat' can often backfire. Besides, there is only one person you would really be cheating and if it is just validation you are seeking for a decision that you have already taken, then just ask your friends, family, the people who know you best. After all, they are likely to give you the answers you want to hear. An accurate psychometric profile, on the other hand, will really help you to understand more about yourself and highlight the areas you may need to work on if you are to become a successful soloist. Of course you may be determined to give it a go even if all the indications are that you are not ideally suited (hopefully the tests will have identified that you are stubborn, determined and wilful!) but at least by having taken them you can better prepare yourself, and your family, for the journey ahead. Remember that the chances are that neither they nor friends, former colleagues etc. will be surprised by the results even if you are, so do not be afraid to ask for their support and understanding. They might even be inclined to offer some practical assistance, and in the early days of becoming your own boss you will want to take every bit of help that is offered. Never turn down any assistance for fear of thinking that it is tantamount to admitting you made a mistake or for fear of looking foolish. People are usually more understanding than you might expect and more generous with their support than you might anticipate. After all, it takes a degree of courage even to attempt to become your own boss.

> 'With realization of one's own potential and self-confidence in one's ability, one can build a better world.'
>
> Dalai Lama

Just remember as you take the psychometric profiling tests that you are doing it for your benefit, no one else's, and no one else need see the results if you prefer them not to. Just answer the questions honestly and accurately, and remember that there are no 'right' or 'wrong' answers. If you have never heard of psychometric profiling or are not sure how useful it really is you might be interested to know that psychometric profile tests are now a fundamental part of recruitment for many large companies, affording employers an insight into personality types of prospective, and current, employees. Indeed, according to the *Guardian* newspaper, more than 95 per cent of the companies in the FTSE 100 use these types of tests to select their employees and many use them to evaluate their employees' ongoing happiness in their jobs.

Insight

Several of the people quoted in this book who have successfully left paid employment to become their own boss did so initially as the result of taking psychometric profiling tests administered by their previous employer, the results of which suggested they would be happier working for themselves!

So you can be pretty sure that these tests really do work and the best ones can deliver a profile which is more accurate than you might like it to be! Tests vary in length and complexity, but most use a set of simple questions to provide an insight into an individual's likely working behaviour. There are a great many different types and styles of psychometric tests, each with their own processes and means of evaluating an individual's behaviour, but they largely follow much the same format – the completion of structured personality questionnaires requiring respondents to answer a number of questions or provide responses to a variety of statements, the responses to which will help you to determine your personality traits and how they fit (or don't fit) the self-employed workplace.

These will include such things as:

- *your approach to your home and work life*
- *your communication style*
- *your strengths and weaknesses regards becoming your own boss*
- *your attitude to work*
- *your ability to get on with others*
- *your motivation, determination and perseverance*
- *your social skills*
- *your preferred working styles*
- *your assertiveness (or lack of it)*
- *your willingness to take instruction and your ability to follow it*
- *your attitude towards authority*
- *how quick you are to make assumptions about other people and the criteria used to do this*
- *your self-reliance*
- *your ability to demonstrate flexibility in your working life and methods.*

It can also help to predict how you might react or perform in various circumstances. The relationships between all these different factors is then interpreted to generate potentially millions of different profiles. Thus these can assist in clarifying what potential career paths may best suit you. If you have a burning desire to leave your job and become your own boss but you really have no idea whether you have a personality and approach to working which suits it (though do remember that there is no one 'right' or even preferable personality type – it is the presence or absence of key traits which is important) then a full psychometric profiling might prove very valuable. For most would-be soloists the decision as to what you would do if you were to become your own boss is the easy part – the difficult part is in deciding whether this sea change is the right career path for you in the first place. Understanding your personality profile and your suitability to becoming your own boss can help you to avoid expensive mistakes as well as giving you the confidence and reassurance that you have every chance of succeeding.

Case study

'Before leaving a very secure, reasonably well-paid career for a much more uncertain existence with potential greater risk (but also greater potential rewards), I carefully weighed my options and considered further employment, but all the psychometric tests pointed me towards the need to work for myself and exploit entrepreneurial aspects of my character.'

Psychometric profiling tests vary widely in cost, but given that you will be using it to help make an informed decision about something as important as your future career you may feel it is worthwhile investing in a good one. They range in price from completely free (although these tend to be online tests analysed straightaway by computer without the often crucial input of a skilled data interpreter, and are often very short with the result that they can be completed quickly and you get the results immediately but with the corresponding loss of accuracy) to several hundreds of pounds (many of them also allow you to take a shorter version free of charge so you can get a feel for them and see if it is likely to be something you will want to pay for). Some can be completed in the comfort of your own home and then sent away for analysis, but the more common option is a residential test administered at a psychometric profiling test centre. These are usually the most accurate and in-depth of all, and also provide the opportunity to discuss the results with an expert who will be able to interpret the data and answer any questions you may have, but they are, of course, the most expensive option.

If you opt for the online version, which is becoming increasingly popular thanks largely to the increasing accuracy of the tests as the interpretive software becomes more and more sophisticated (although in general they still lag some way behind a residential test), then you will find no shortage of choices just a few clicks away. Simply search for 'psychometric profiling tests' and you will be presented with numerous options.

The beauty of a psychometric profiling test administered by an expert is the accuracy of the output derived from skilled analysis of all the data. It is therefore impossible to achieve the same level of accuracy or indeed complexity taking a simple pen and paper psychometric profiling test, but some facilitated soul-searching and self-examination will provide a good starting point and an indication of your suitability to going solo and becoming your own boss.

Use the list of questions and statements on the following pages as stimulus to begin to understand some of your work-related aptitudes and attitudes. See which apply to you and which do not, and in either case whether it is marginal or acute. Give yourself a score from 1 to 5 for each, 1 being the most marginal and 5 being the strongest.

Hopefully once you have completed the exercise you will have a clearer idea of some of your work-related strengths and weaknesses, desires and dislikes, and a firmer idea of whether or not you think taking the leap to becoming your own boss is the best course of action for you at this stage. If you think that it is, then why not arrange to take a full psychometric profiling test to help you to see exactly where your strengths and weaknesses might lie?

Group 1
- ☐ You are self-motivated.
- ☐ You are a risk taker.
- ☐ You enjoy an occasional gamble.
- ☐ You have the support of immediate family in your business life.
- ☐ You are naturally analytical.

Group 2
- ☐ You work best with standard work patterns.
- ☐ You are a creature of habit.
- ☐ You work best with external stimulus.
- ☐ You enjoy social company during your working day.
- ☐ You need security.

Group 3
- ☐ You are a good communicator.
- ☐ You can make difficult decisions quickly and easily.
- ☐ You are a natural leader.
- ☐ You are organized.
- ☐ You are a problem solver.

Group 4
- ☐ You need stability.
- ☐ You enjoy managing other people.
- ☐ You dislike isolation.
- ☐ You like to work the same hours each day.
- ☐ You really appreciate having your efforts recognized.

Group 5
- ☐ You prefer to work with minimal supervision.
- ☐ You are assertive.
- ☐ You are confident.
- ☐ You are calm in a crisis.
- ☐ You have bags of enthusiasm for your ventures.

Group 6
- ☐ You are imaginative.
- ☐ You demonstrate initiative on a regular basis.

- [ ] You are resourceful.
- [ ] You are willing to learn.
- [ ] It annoys you if you cannot see a project through to the end.

Group 7
- [ ] Are you always prepared for any eventuality?
- [ ] Are you sometimes told you are bossy?
- [ ] Do you crave change on a regular basis?
- [ ] Do you work well under pressure?
- [ ] Are you good at multi-tasking?

Group 8
- [ ] Do you often find yourself running out of time?
- [ ] Do you often have a guilty conscience?
- [ ] Do you wish you were more efficient?
- [ ] Do you dislike having to 'sell yourself'?
- [ ] Are you introverted?

Now add together your scores from groups 1, 3, 5, 6 and 7.
Group 1:
Group 3:
Group 5:
Group 6:
Group 7:
Total:

This is your total for section 'A'
Now add together your total scores from groups 2, 4 and 8.
Group 2:
Group 4:
Group 8:
Total:

This is your total for section 'B'
Lastly, subtract your total for section 'B' from your total for section 'A'. This gives you your final score.

(Contd)

Total for section 'A':
Total for section 'B':
Final score:

Compare your final score to the chart below to see how you might fare as your own boss:

−50 to 0: You show very few signs of being a natural candidate to become your own boss. Is it time to reconsider your options?

1 to 50: You show limited aptitude to becoming your own boss. Are you clear about your reasons for wanting to take the leap?

51 to 75: You certainly have some of the aptitude necessary to be successful as your own boss, but is it enough?

76 to 100: You demonstrate a good degree of natural aptitude to becoming your own boss. This is certainly an option you should actively explore.

101 to 110: You are a natural go-getter very well suited to becoming your own boss. What are you waiting for?!

Future paths

It's decision time. You have decided to quit your old job, or it has quit you, and now you have the opportunity to forge a new career path. So what will it be? Firstly you need to decide whether you want to stay doing the same sort of work or something very similar, or whether you want to take the opportunity to embrace a completely new career. There are four basic choices:

a) *same sort of work but with a different company*
b) *different sort of work within the same company*
c) *different sort of work with a different company*
d) *same sort of work or different sort of work but going solo.*

Each of these provides a different route to a new career but offers varying degrees of safety and security versus adventure and new challenges.

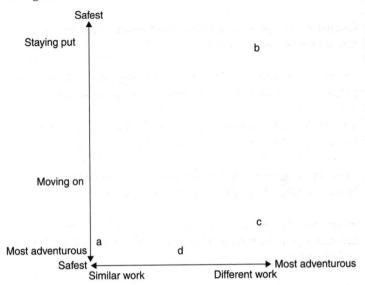

a) Same sort of work but with a different company

If becoming your own boss is not the right option for you, or at least not at the moment, then it may be worth exploring the possibility of moving to a different company in a similar field. They may be in a position to offer you some of the elements you crave in your current job (but know you will not be able to get if you stay where you are), while at the same time providing a degree of work routine stability. It is sometimes said that a change is as good as a rest and certainly moving to a new company can provide you with a new perspective and a new set of challenges and perhaps afford you the opportunity to do something different. Use your network of contacts as well as the internet as research resources and see what sort of work might be available and where. It may well be that a move to a smaller company, for instance, affords you more freedom, gives you more responsibility and puts you more in charge of your own destiny (depending on the size of the company, your experience, and how keen the bosses of the new company are to have you on board you may even be able to become a partner at some stage), while a move to a larger company might offer better promotion prospects or further training.

b) Different sort of work within the same company
If your dissatisfaction with your job stems not from being in someone else's employ but with the work itself, and if when you look realistically at your options you decide that staying with your current employer might actually be your best option (perhaps because it is 'better the devil you know'), then your best option might be to change your job *within* the same company. Of course this depends to a large degree on the size of the company and the nature of the work undertaken but it is always worth having a frank conversation with your bosses to see what your options are. After all, if they are pleased with your work and want to keep you as an employee then it is in their best interests to ensure you are happy and motivated and it might not require a huge change – often just a small difference in your day-to-day working life can make all the difference to the way you feel about it.

c) Different sort of work with a different company
If, after some rigorous soul-searching, you decide that you need a really quite substantial change in your work life then it may be time to consider moving to a different company *and* taking a position which involves a different type of work. Be aware however that this can be very difficult to achieve all in one go; you are, after all, expecting an employer to whom you are new (and something of an unknown quantity) to take you on in a role which will be new to you, one in which you may have little or no experience. Often this sort of step-change is best accomplished in two stages: either move to a new employer but in a role with which you are familiar, and then when they have got to know you discuss the possibility of changing your role within the company, or stay where you are for the time being but change the type of work you do, and when you have gained some experience in your new role you will be better placed to approach a new company about doing the same job for them. In this way you can see that it is usually best to start with option a) or b), even if option c) is your

ultimate goal; equally, by starting with a more modest and more immediately achievable aim you will put yourself in a position where you can test the waters so that although you may have set out with option a) or b) in mind, having achieved this you may then decide to push through to option c), and you will be perfectly placed to do so.

d) Same sort of work or different sort of work but going solo

This is of course the most fundamental change and it may be best to focus your new career and your new business in a field familiar to you, at least initially, but either way it is the very fact that you are now your own boss which will provide the biggest differences to your work life.

Of course only you will know which of these represents the right approach for you, according to the needs of your situation, your personality type and so on, but hopefully by now you will have a good idea of who and where you are now and, most importantly, who and where you want to be.

> **'He who is outside his door has the hardest part of his journey behind him.'**
>
> (Dutch proverb)

You should also have a clearer idea of whether or not you want to quit your job and take the leap to becoming your own boss at this juncture.

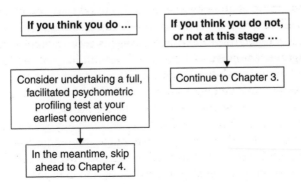

KEY THINGS TO REMEMBER

▶ *Be brutally honest with yourself and try to determine whether or not you have the right type of personality to make it as your own boss.*

▶ *Identify any additions to your skill set which will be necessary/beneficial in making the transition to becoming your own boss, and plan how and when you are going to acquire these.*

▶ *Identify any support you may need in making the transition to becoming your own boss and ascertain who will be able to provide this for you.*

▶ *Determine your work-related strengths and weaknesses and highlight those areas in which you need to improve.*

▶ *A psychometric profiling test can be invaluable in helping you to determine whether or not the move to becoming your own boss is right for you.*

▶ *Identifying your key personality traits and understanding who you are, and who you want to be, is vital to making a smooth and successful transition from paid employment to becoming your own boss.*

▶ *Identify your key work-related aptitudes and attitudes.*

▶ *Consider the options of staying with your current employer but changing your job or doing the same sort of work but in a different company.*

3

....

Staying put

In this chapter you will learn:
- *about how to improve your situation – and your salary*
- *about working from home*
- *how to shake up your working life*

How to improve your situation – and your salary

> **'Men are anxious to improve their circumstances, but are unwilling to improve themselves.'**
>
> James Allen

Going solo is not for everyone. It can be hard work, lonely and uncertain, and for many people the dream of becoming their own boss is far better than the reality. If, having taken stock of your situation and weighed all your options – and having been completely, even brutally honest with yourself – you have come to the conclusion that becoming your own boss and working for yourself is not right for you, or at least not at the moment, then deciding to stay put may well be the best and the bravest decision you could take. What this does not mean, however, is that you have to resign yourself to going back to your old job and picking up exactly where you left off with all the same old niggles and drawbacks as before. Having come this far, and having looked at the option of leaving your job (a fairly drastic step) then it is safe to assume that all is not as good as it could be with your employer. You have taken a significant step away from your job in considering leaving it, and this distance affords you the benefit of gaining real perspective on your situation; so use this new-found insight to help you determine what it is you dislike about your current work life, what dissatisfies or disappoints you, what you feel is lacking, and what you feel you need to implement in order to achieve a more satisfying and rewarding career. Now that you have the advantage of having gained this perspective and insight, you have a great opportunity to make any changes you feel are necessary, be they minor tweaks or major step-changes; you might even feel that now is the right time to switch jobs and move to another company, perhaps even in another industry; or you may decide that identifying and implementing some key changes in your current job will improve your work life to the degree necessary to make you want to stay.

Insight

If you decide to stay put and implement some changes in your current work life, then now is also an excellent time to renegotiate your situation with your employer and improve your salary/benefits package in the ways which are most important to you; it may be an improved position within the company, and improved salary, an increase in your holiday entitlement, or even just a better job title (to many people this is the most important of all!).

Ask to have a meeting with your boss and tell them that you are seriously considering leaving. After all, if your boss knows you are seriously thinking of leaving then it puts you in a very strong negotiating position (assuming of course that you are good at your job and that they would want to keep you!). They do not need to know when you made your decision and that you have already decided to stay, and the moment they know you are committed (or resigned) to staying, your position of strength goes out the window, so negotiate a better salary *before* 'deciding' to stay.

Before you have this meeting you will also need to have determined those elements of your work life which need to change. Use the following exercise to help you to determine what these are. It will take some time to do this properly and will require some rigorous soul-searching to really understand what you want and need from your career for it to be really satisfying and meaningful – but it is time well spent.

> '**My friend, saying that you don't have time to improve your thoughts and your life is like saying you don't have time to stop for gas because you are too busy driving. Eventually it will catch up with you.**'
>
> (author unknown)

Firstly, draw up a list of all the things about your job which you dislike and which could reasonably be altered for the better. If you are a butcher, there is no point in saying that you do not like dealing with meat, but if it is one particular meat you find difficult or boring to work with, or if it is interfacing with the customers, dealing with the finances, etc. then perhaps there is a way to avoid, or at the very least to minimize these in your day-to-day routine.

Some of the most common negative aspects people quote in relation to their job are:

- ▶ *feeling underpaid*
- ▶ *feeling undervalued*
- ▶ *being stressed*
- ▶ *operating in a poor working environment*
- ▶ *putting up with difficult working hours*
- ▶ *having a poor relationship with their boss or line manager*
- ▶ *having a poor relationship with their colleagues*
- ▶ *disliking the office politics*
- ▶ *finding the work unchallenging or boring*
- ▶ *feeling stuck in a rut*
- ▶ *not being able to see any future progression which inspires them*
- ▶ *feeling that they are not fulfilling their potential*
- ▶ *feeling that they are wasting their life away*
- ▶ *knowing that they do not want to be in the same position in ten years' time.*

Of course your list may be entirely different, but it is likely that at least some of the above points will sound familiar, if not all of them! (If you find yourself starting a third page though, you will probably have already discovered that it is time to move on!) Once your list is complete, divide it into three sections:

Crucial: those elements which simply have to change if things are to get any better and without which your work life situation will be untenable.

Secondary: the things you could live with or without if push comes to shove but which would make a real difference if they could be addressed.

Would be nice ...: all the other points, which are more niggles than real problems but if they could be fixed then so much the better.

Next, draw up a second list, this time of all the things about your job which you like just as they are, and those which you like but which could be improved still further and categorize them into three levels of importance just as you did with your first list.

Now draw up a third list – this is your wish list. Again, the goals need to be attainable (most of us would like an on-site spa with complimentary massages and perhaps free drinks but it is probably not very realistic to hope for) and if you have got an idea of timescale or ways in which your ideas could be incorporated then include these as well. Lastly, divide this list into three levels of importance just as you did with the other two.

By now you will have three lists, each divided into three levels of priority. The first thing to do is to put aside both the second list and those parts of the first and third lists which contain those elements that are of secondary and tertiary levels of importance to you. Do not throw them away because they will be useful to you at a later date, once you have sorted out those things which are your more immediate priorities. For now though you should concentrate your efforts solely on the primary sections of the first and third lists. These detail all those aspects which are crucially important to you; those which you absolutely must change in order for your work life to improve significantly and those which, if they can be implemented, will really improve your work life so that your job becomes something you enjoy and not something you just tolerate. By comparing these two sections of your first and third lists, you can see at a glance the things which you feel really need to be improved and what the dream scenario for your job looks like. Next, you need to go through each of the points on these two sub-lists and try to determine how easy or difficult each is likely to be to implement and the time frame over which any changes can be brought about.

Now draw a simple two-axes graph on which to plot the points. On the X axis chart the degree of difficulty (time and/or effort required) of achieving each of your aims and on the Y axis rate the level of importance, so that something which you feel is crucial but difficult or slow to implement will be in the top right corner and something which is less important and easier/quicker to implement will be in the lower left corner.

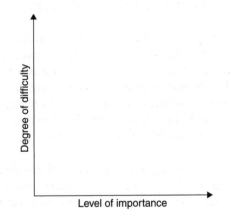

Now draw a line vertically down the middle of the chart and another horizontally across the middle, dividing the chart into four quarters. This determines for you the order in which things need to be tackled:

The bottom right-hand corner: This quadrant contains those elements which are most important to you and which are the easiest to tackle and quickest to implement. These should be your first priority.

The bottom left-hand corner: This quadrant contains those elements which are quick and easy to implement but do not hold the same level of importance for you. However, bearing in mind that this chart only contains those elements that you rated 'crucial' to begin with, they still hold a high level of importance for you. These should be your second priority.

The top right-hand corner: This quadrant contains those elements which will be difficult to achieve or will take a long time to implement but are nevertheless very important to you. These should be your third priority.

The top left-hand corner: This quadrant contains those elements which are of a lesser importance to you and will take a long time to implement or be difficult to achieve. These should be your fourth priority.

Now that you have clearly defined and prioritized all the changes you need to implement in your work life in order to make it really work for you, you will need to ascertain the approximate lengths of time it will take to achieve each of them. This is important because it allows you to monitor the progress in your work life thereby allowing you to see whether or not things really are improving in the way and at the speed you need them to. It is far too easy, having got this far, to feel that by having identified all the changes that need to take place you are halfway there and that by starting the process of implementing the changes you will complete the picture. Unfortunately the reality is that each of your changes will almost certainly need to be carefully managed all the way through from implementation to completion, and identifying a timescale will ensure you can keep things on track. If, after a reasonable period of time, you look back at your list and realize that none of the changes have really taken place and that there is no good reason for this then you will need to weigh up your options once more. If the barriers to your work life becoming as you need it to be are being created through foot-dragging by senior management, or worse, by a concerted effort to deliberately introduce roadblocks, then you will need to consider the possibility that these changes will never take place and that perhaps leaving your job is the only way in which you will ever really gain genuine satisfaction from your career.

'If you must play, decide on three things at the start: the rules of the game, the stakes, and the quitting time.'

(Chinese proverb)

Working from home

If you decide that jumping ship is not for you, or at least not at the moment, but that part of the problem lies in the commute, the office politics, the working environment etc., or if you just feel that not having to go into the office every day would shake things up sufficiently to give your day-to-day working a new lease of life, then one possible solution is to work from home. Of course this is not possible for everybody, but many people who assume it would not be possible or practical for them are surprised to find that an enlightened boss can help them to make it work, even if only for one or two days per week – and that might be enough to make all the difference.

Case study

'Working from home makes me feel so much more connected to my life away from work, even when I'm working! Although I still have to go to the office two to three days per week, having those extra days without all the hassles of the commute, and being able to collect the children from school etc., makes all the difference.'

You might even be able to get some assistance with setting up a suitable IT workstation in your home to help ensure your absence from the office causes minimal disruption. For many companies, it is not the idea of their employees working from home which they dislike, it is the fact that they will not be able to contact them quickly and easily whenever they need to, that important meetings will go unattended, that some vital documents will not be immediately accessible or that your knowledge and expertise will not be readily available and so on. Fortunately, however, none of that holds true in today's world of instant and everywhere communication; email, Skype, improved mobile network coverage and bandwidth, conference calling and video calling, IM and so on have revolutionized the way in which we can reach and be reached, and using them smartly should enable many people to work from home, at least part time. And from your company's point of view they stand to gain from a cost saving in energy usage together with a reduced carbon footprint with your reduced commute, not to mention a much happier and more motivated member of staff, so it really should be a win-win situation. Just remember that you will need to make some major adjustments to your home space and your work routines in order to accommodate working from home.

Case study

'I was very prepared functionally, but I think I was still unprepared for the actual working at home bit – being in my own home each day with nowhere to go. That was tough to get used to at first. I would sometimes make a big fuss about going up to town with my briefcase etc. only to sit in a Starbucks and do more emails. It was a bit crazy, but it worked for me!'

Shaking up your working life

Another important way in which you can help to improve your working life is to influence the hours you work; not how many, but which specific hours they are, and even the number of days over which those hours are spread. If your standard working day is seven and a half hours and you have a fifty-minute commute each way, then by working from home just two days per week you save three hours and twenty minutes of travel time, time which you can use to get some work done. So by adding just one hour onto each working day from Monday to Thursday you will have completed your working week one day early. And this does not just give you one fewer day to work, it gives you one extra day's break.

Insight

Although the reduction in your working week is a modest 20 per cent, the increase in your week's leisure time is a whopping 50 per cent. That's 50 per cent more time to do with as you wish, to stop living at work and start working at living.

Imagine that your salary was suddenly increased by 50 per cent and you begin to realize the true value of the additional time. With very little effort you are improving your work/life balance from 5/2 to 4/3, a huge improvement in anyone's book. Not only that, but you have extended your weekend by a day, turning it into a long weekend. Suddenly it is a much more usable period of time, long enough to take a trip away or to really get stuck into that job you have been putting off for far too long because it is not worth getting everything set up to tackle it only to have to put it all away again before you really get started.

So, if you have decided that your best option really is to stay in your current job, or to seek similar employment elsewhere, then by shaking up your routine and thinking outside the conventional working week box you can improve your lot to a considerable degree.

'The biggest room in the world is the room for improvement.'

(author unknown)

KEY THINGS TO REMEMBER

▶ *There is no disgrace if, after some rigorous soul-searching, you come to the conclusion that taking the leap to becoming your own boss is not right for you, or at least not at the moment.*

▶ *Use the perspective you have gained through considering quitting your job to understand more fully what you need to change in your current work life situation to give yourself the career you really want.*

▶ *Prioritize the changes you need to implement and draw up a plan, with a timescale, to achieve this.*

▶ *Make the most of this opportunity to renegotiate your situation (position within the company, salary, holiday entitlement, title etc.).*

▶ *Working from home part time really is viable for the majority of people. If you think this might provide the required stimulus to your work life, then talk to your boss about ways in which the company can help you to implement it – and stress to them the benefits it will provide to the company.*

▶ *Changing the specific hours you work and the number of days over which these are spread can really help you to shake up your working life.*

4

Quitting your job

In this chapter you will learn:
- *when is the best time to move on*
- *how to derive maximum benefit from quitting*
- *about what steps you can take for 'leaving well'*
- *how to strengthen your ties and the importance of contacts*
- *how to check your employment contract*
- *how to set up your business* **before** *you take the leap*

'Those who initiate change will have a better opportunity to manage the change that is inevitable.'

William Pollard

When to move on

It is very unlikely that you will ever find yourself in the position of having completely run out of challenges in your work life, but you know it is time to move on when you do not find the challenges you are being given interesting and energizing, when you know you cannot or will not get promoted in the foreseeable future so the challenges are unlikely to become more stimulating, and when you feel that no matter how many political manoeuvres you make or how much you shout at your boss things are not going to improve much, or in the way that you need them to. It is also a pretty big clue when you simply cannot see yourself doing what you are doing for the next five, ten or twenty years. Another good indicator, as well as an excellent motivating factor, is when you see others in your industry who have left to become their own boss and are doing so successfully so you know that it is possible – especially if you know in your heart of hearts that you are better at your job than they are at theirs!

Case study

'I acquired full industry knowledge as head of touring for a major theatre producer. After five years there, I felt it was the time to seek a different challenge and was offered a role as a producer/creative for a television company. This was offered on a freelance basis initially, which opened the door for me to start up my own theatre company to run alongside the television work. There was no conflict of interest, so that was fine, and I had been asked time and time again during my years in my former job whether I would consider booking/managing theatre tours away from their shows. I wouldn't and couldn't do so then, now I could. It also meant that ten years of theatre would not go to waste.'

If you are interested and excited by seeing others do what you do, but as their own boss, and if you feel that your job has reached a dead-end, then you might well conclude that it is time to quit and try your hand at going solo. For many people, becoming their own boss means carrying on with much the same work as they were employed to do, only this time they will be taking all the risks and keeping all the rewards. For others, it provides the opportunity to leave the work they have been doing and start doing something completely different, perhaps turning a hobby into a profitable enterprise. The advent of new communication technologies has allowed people to trade simply, quickly and efficiently from their home, be it buying and selling on eBay, producing goods to sell through their own dedicated or third-party website, or a great many other business models. You may even be leaving your erstwhile employer with the long-term goal of beginning a new career in a different field, but you know that this will probably take a long time to achieve and be less profitable in the interim than sticking to the same type of work. However, by becoming your own boss in a similar field to the one which you are leaving you may have the flexibility to focus on getting a new career path up to speed. It may be possible to devote four days a week to your new business whilst leaving you one day free to concentrate on building a completely new business structure, perhaps turning a hobby into your new full-time career. So taking the leap to becoming your own boss in a less preferred but more immediately viable arena might be just what you need to give you the time and space to develop your hobby into a full-time career, allowing you to become your own boss in just the way you want to. Importantly, it can give you the option and opportunity to give things a go, to earn your money while you experiment and see whether it really is a viable option – before you take the leap. Remaining working for a big corporate company, on the other hand, would never have allowed you the time and space, or flexibility, to develop your hobby in this way.

Whatever your reasons and your ultimate goals, one thing remains true for the majority of situations – that your former employer will be able to give you some much needed support as you first start to go solo, provided that you leave well. How easily such support translates from your old employment to your new working life will depend to a great extent on how similar the two may be, but even if they seem to have little or nothing in common it is still very likely that by parting on good terms you will be doing yourself a big favour – even if it is the last thing you feel like doing!

So, if having looked at all the pros and cons of staying in gainful employment versus quitting your job and going solo, you have reached the conclusion that setting up on your own really is for you, then it is time to work out a strategy for leaving.

'If at first you don't succeed, try, try again. Then quit. There's no use being a damn fool about it.'

W.C. Fields

Deriving maximum benefit from quitting

So, you have decided to quit your job – but what is the optimum time for leaving? For many people this is one of the most difficult decisions they face; not whether they should move on but when to do so. Timing is everything, but there is never a 'right' time and in all probability there will never be a good time. It is up to you therefore to create the opportunity.

Having decided the time has definitely come to move on, you need to engineer a process for leaving well – and it is crucial, always, to leave on good terms even if what you really feel like doing is sticking two fingers up at your bosses and telling them where they can go. You need to leave in such a way that they are desperate for you to stay; that way if and when you do leave they will always be keen for you to return, crucial if you discover further down the line that becoming your own boss is not for you. This is the easiest fallback plan you can put in place, and do not fall into the trap of thinking that by having a fallback plan should being your own boss not work out as well as you had hoped you are being negative and diminishing your chances of success. Only a fool would deliberately burn bridges they did not need to, and you certainly need to have thought through your options should you need to return to paid employment.

Case study

'You always need to have a fallback plan. Mine was going back to the company I left in order to become my own boss, and still remains so even to this day. If for whatever reason it suddenly all goes horribly wrong you need to know that all you have to do is pick up the phone and your previous employer will welcome you back with open arms.'

So, by leaving your job well with your bosses eager for you to stay and parting with the company on good terms, you know that if the worst comes to the worst you can always return at any point in the future because a seat there will always be kept warm for you.

Steps for leaving well

In engineering the process for leaving well, on good and friendly terms with your bosses and your colleagues, the first conversation you have should not be one in which you tell them that you are leaving, but one in which you tell them that you are seriously considering leaving. In other words, you are opening a mature conversation *not about leaving but about your future*. This is vitally important because you simply never know what people are going to say and it can be extraordinary what comes out of it.

Case study

'After 14 good years with the same company I had been promoted as far as I could reasonably have expected to have been and I felt the time had come to move on. I was sure I had exhausted all possibilities for a challenging and satisfying career with my current employers and I had thoroughly researched the opportunities for becoming my own boss. I felt it prudent, however, to broach the subject as tactfully as I could and, although I had pretty much made up my mind what I was going to do, I presented my leaving as just one of the options I was considering. My bosses were very understanding, thanked me for my courtesy and asked me to give them a couple of weeks to consider what I had told them. At the end of the week the managing director asked to see me, expressed his concern at my potential departure, and asked me if I would be interested

(Contd)

in going to Australia for three years to set up and run a new branch of the company in Melbourne. This threw me for a complete loop as there had been no indication that the company intended to open a new office, let alone one on the other side of the world! For me, however, this would be a dream come true and it took me all of 30 seconds to make up my mind to stay with the company and pack my bags for Australia.'

So it is always worth being open and honest with your bosses and telling them that you have outgrown your job, that you do not like the way your job is, that you are not happy in your work and so on, and detailing the reasons why, to see what they say. You never know, they might just come up with the answer to your prayers and, even if it is only a five per cent chance, at least you will know that you have covered all your bases and there will not be any nasty lingering, nagging doubts that maybe you would have been better off staying. It is worth bearing in mind that the grass is always greener on the other side and never is this more true than when quitting your job to become your own boss; as soon as you have gone solo you will be presented with so many new challenges, intractable problems and seemingly insurmountable headaches that at times the idea of still being in salaried employ can seem very tempting. Of course you will also be presented with a great many unexpected opportunities, freedoms you had not envisaged and surprising bonuses in different shapes and sizes, but for those moments when it all seems like it is just too much hard work it is really important that you know you explored all the possibilities for remaining where you were and none were sufficiently tempting to make you want to stay. That way, when the doubts over your new career as your own boss start to creep in, you can banish them quickly by reminding yourself that you really did exhaust all the possibilities for staying put.

'Our doubts are traitors and make us lose the good we oft might win by fearing to attempt.'

William Shakespeare

Also, you have not presented your desire to leave as a *fait accompli* but you have been completely transparent and fair, giving your employers every opportunity to retain your services, should they wish to do so. Hopefully by opening a mature discussion about your desire to leave you will get to the truth about what they value about you and this will help you to better understand your strengths in the workplace which in turn will help you to focus more clearly on exactly what your offer should be if and when you do become your own boss, and in which areas you might need to improve. You are then able to leave on good terms having listened to all the offers put to you, and your employers will hopefully respect the fact that you gave them every chance to retain you. Importantly they will understand *why* you feel the need to leave and it is worthwhile making the point to them that it is something you feel you need to do – you have to try going solo or you will always regret it, rather than that you are leaving because you can no longer stand working there (even if that happens to be the truth!).

Strengthening ties

Unless you are making the move to becoming your own boss in order to pursue a career in something which you currently enjoy only as a hobby, the chances are you will find yourself working in a broadly similar field to the one in which you have plied your trade whilst in paid employment. This is true of the majority of people who make the move to becoming their own boss. Few and far between are the people who are desperate to become their own boss and who have spent years working in accountancy only to decide to make the leap to solo working as a tree surgeon, or been gainfully employed as a photographer their whole career and then decide to become their own boss as a plumber. Most people elect to stay within the industry they know, which of course makes a lot of sense. The motivation to becoming their own boss is not to radically change career paths but to be able to call the shots, to make the rules and keep all the profits.

One of the best routes, although not available to everybody, is to agree with your bosses a structure for making your leaving a gradual process so that from the clients' point of view you are not simply there one minute and gone the next but rather that you fade out gradually. Perhaps your bosses are worried that a key client might feel shaky if you suddenly drop off the radar and so you might agree to continue working a couple of days a week, at an agreed day rate, just on that client. This again bolsters your approach to leaving well as it aids your erstwhile employer while at the same time guaranteeing some very welcome income for your new company over the tricky first few months. Crucially, this means that you still have a foot in the door, that you are still around once you have left albeit in a virtual sense, and you have every reason to be in regular contact with your old company and all your ex-colleagues. Once this period has been completed, or from the outset if this avenue is not open to you, it is important to identify a few key people at your old company with whom you will remain in regular contact.

Try as much as possible to get invited to the odd company social occasion; it is amazing what you can discover to your advantage and how much future work you can secure over a company Christmas lunch! Stay friendly, keep rubbing shoulders with your ex-employers, keep the lines of communication open and make sure you do not just disappear in a puff of smoke so that no one ever hears from you again.

One of the key things to be aware of is that if someone you rate in your old company is moving on, it can impact on your business, either positively or negatively. If they are moving to another company, agency etc. then you will have an instant *entrée* to a whole new source of work. If on the other hand they have decided to follow your fine example and set up as their own boss then they may well be in direct competition with you. By being in regular contact you will at least get plenty of warning. Better yet, you might be able to suggest to them that you join forces in some way, either actually working together or working separately but in tandem to ensure that you avoid negatively impacting on each other's business. You might even be able to put some work each other's way from time to time if one of you finds that you are in the enviable position of being offered more work than you can manage.

Contacts

One of the most important things you can do when you leave your job to become your own boss is to make a list of all the people you have ever worked with, all your clients and potential clients. Why? Because now you are on your own you need to compile your own database. No doubt you will have relied on having a comprehensive database to hand whilst in paid employment and now that you are going solo you will need to start your own database of every potential source of work – email addresses and phone numbers, the best times to contact them, their preferred method of communication and so on.

Checking your employment contract

Before you leave your job, get hold of a copy of your employment contract and get it reviewed by an employment lawyer. They will explain the salient points to you and make sure that you understand your obligations to your employer once you have left as well as any limitations you may be under. This is particularly important if you are setting up business in an area where client confidentiality is a sensitive issue and non-compete clauses are *de rigueur*. Do not be tempted to think you are the one person who can get away without having your employment contract checked by an expert; it can save you a lot of time, money, and headaches further down the line. No matter how well your new business venture goes, if you have been working for a large multinational it is highly unlikely that you will ever have as much money or as many lawyers as they do, so do your homework and make sure you avoid any unnecessary confrontation. It may even throw up some surprises to your advantage ...

Case study

'I had always understood that if and when I quit my job to become my own boss I would be unable to work with any of my previous employers' clients for a period of two years. I took this to mean that for a period of two years from the date of my leaving I wouldn't be able to accept any paid work from any of them. I was pretty clear on this but thought it prudent to double check anyway and sought the services of an employment lawyer. They reviewed my employment contract and informed me that in fact this was not the case. In actual fact my contract forbade me to work with any of the clients with whom I had worked during the previous two years from the date of leaving. At first the difference seemed subtle, but I immediately set about scrolling through my contacts database and I was amazed just how many clients I knew and had talked to regularly but hadn't actually undertaken any paid work for in the last two years. I had successfully completed projects for them prior to this so they knew me and knew my work, and I had remained in contact with them so I knew what their plans were and where there might be an opportunity for me to help as soon as I set up my own business, but as I hadn't actually worked for them in the last two years I was perfectly entitled to contact them to try to secure work the very first day I became my own boss. So it was open season ...'

It is very useful to understand exactly what the terms of your contract constitute and also to understand which elements are enforceable. Since in most countries there are legal measures to protect a person's trade from undue restriction, a great many employment contracts include terms and conditions which are advantageous to the employer but which do not stand up to scrutiny and have actually been included more in hope than expectation! Since these are not enforceable in a court of law you can feel free to ignore them; just be sure you are very clear as to which these are. Also bear in mind that while you may not be able to work for particular clients for a certain period of time there is nothing to prevent you staying in contact with them, so be sure you do.

Setting up your business *before* you take the leap

Before you leave your job there is a whole raft of things you need to get set up for your new business in order to make sure that you hit the ground running from day one and do not spend the first weeks as your own boss chasing your tail because you were not sufficiently prepared. Chief among these are:

- *a company bank account*
- *company credit cards*
- *company cheque books and paying in books*
- *a new mobile phone for your business*
- *a fax machine with a dedicated line*
- *a workable office set up (a good desk and a comfortable chair will make a huge difference to how you feel)*
- *a dedicated telephone landline*
- *any stationery you might require including business cards and headed paper*
- *a plentiful supply of paper, pens, post-it notes, printer ink, flipcharts etc.*
- *high-speed Internet access*
- *a web cam for Skypeing.*

It may seem unnecessary to be arranging all these things at this early stage, before your company is up and running, but it is absolutely crucial – if you do not have a company bank account you cannot bill your first client (or second or third) and without this your business is going nowhere, financially at least. It also makes a real difference to your clients' perception of your business and your abilities if they receive an invoice on headed company paper inviting them to submit their payment directly into your company bank account rather than receiving scant details on a blank piece of A4 asking for a cheque.

Insight

Not having your new business banking set up before you actively become your own boss means you will be spending money without the means to acquire any – a guaranteed route to negative equity.

If you are not going to work from home but have decided instead to rent some office space, then make sure you take the time and trouble to scope it out before you leave your job. Not only do you need to find the space you wish to rent and get a rental agreement in place, but you also need to plan the layout of your new office and arrange for everything you will require to be delivered there and installed ready for your arrival. In this way you can ensure that the transition from being employed to becoming your own boss is super smooth. You need to make sure that you can leave your job at six o'clock on the Wednesday evening and be in your office, sat at your desk, with your new phone and new computer plumbed in and ready to go at nine o'clock Thursday morning.

TAKING THE LEAP

'Mere change is not growth. Growth is the synthesis of change and continuity, and where there is no continuity there is no growth.'

C.S. Lewis

In order to derive maximum benefit from making the transition from paid employment to becoming your own boss you need to take advantage of as many aids your previous employer can give you as possible. The closer your new career will be to your old career the easier it is to see how this might work; if you have spent the last 20 years working for a firm of accountants and you are a trained accountant planning to set up your own business as an accountant then it is pretty easy to see the cross-over; indeed, the biggest challenge might be in that you cannot take any of your previous clients with you. What you can get, however, is a ready-made support network of people in the same boat and who have a lot of experience of successfully running an accountancy firm, details of all the suppliers they use and have found to be reliable and trustworthy, an established firm who can recommend you and perhaps even provide you with work from time to time when they have more business than they can handle and so on.

But supposing you are leaving your job to begin your solo career in a completely different field? How can you use your former employer to help you to establish your new business? Let us suppose for example that you have been working for a local catering firm and you now want to go solo to start making your living from your hobby of designing and making dolls' houses. On the face of it the two jobs have nothing in common and so it will be nigh on impossible to gain any advantage from your previous employment. But some logical thinking, followed by some lateral thinking, plus a good deal of creative 'out of the box' thinking creates a template for deriving business advantages from leaving well.

CONTACTS AND NETWORKING

Never underestimate how important this is in practically any and every sphere of business.

> ### Case study
>
> 'We all network at big corporate companies – who's who, promotions etc. – but when you are solo it becomes a key skill for survival. It's critical for finding clients as well as suppliers/colleagues to work with as well as (and for me a really important one) people to chat to and share your daily thoughts with. Suddenly LinkedIn (I never could get on with Facebook or Twitter) becomes a source of reassurance: I am not alone, other people think I'm OK, other people are doing this solo thing too.'

You need to sell your dolls' houses and for that you need customers. Your previous employer has a raft of customers with whom, crucially, they have an established relationship. Of course not all of these customers are necessarily going to want a dolls' house, but you know that in the early stages of setting up and establishing your business not only will you need to engage in some targeted marketing and sales but you will also need to find ways simply to cast enough bread on the water to start getting in those all important orders. So if your erstwhile employer has a couple of thousand customers then it is fairly likely that at least a few of those might be interested in purchasing a dolls' house. Moreover, each potential customer can reach several more people, so already there is a sizable customer base being advertised to and, by providing suitable sales material, they can begin to spread the word on your behalf. Also, if the catering firm knows a bit about its customers, and even its suppliers, then you can engage in some careful targeting using this knowledge. Once you have started to get a response you can distil the information to further refine your targeting.

Sharing a client base

Once you begin to develop your own network and contacts you will be in a position to feed back some information to your former employer to help them. Of course you will need to be careful that the information you are sharing does not breach any confidences or fall foul of any rules or regulations, such as the Data Protection Act, but it is really important to try to make sure that the relationship is genuinely two-way if it is to be valuable in the long term.

Reputation

Borrowing equity from your previous employer can be invaluable. If they enjoy a good reputation then so can you, right from the off. Just make sure that your former employer is happy for you to cash in on their good name and that everyone knows your provenance and your history.

Printing

The sales material provided might include business cards, flyers, price lists, photos of current models, technical specifications and so on. These all need to be printed which can be a major cost, especially when starting out. Having parted on good terms with your previous employer, however, it is very likely that they will be able to help you; they are almost certain to have contacts with a good printer and quite possibly have negotiated a good deal for regular business too, so an introduction here can save you a good deal of money as well as a lot of time, at the same time ensuring that the company to which you are entrusting the production of your promotional materials, the business image you are presenting to the world, is one which you know to be excellent – all of which are hugely important as you begin your new career.

Website
Unless you are a dab hand at web design you will need to get a professional to do this for you, and also to maintain it to ensure it is always up-to-date and relevant. Your former employer will probably know of a good, relatively inexpensive web designer and an introduction might furnish you with preferential rates. The designer may well give you a good price for being given the job of designing all your materials including those for print and a company logo where appropriate, too, further reducing your costs.

Trade fairs
Visiting local trade fairs and showing off your wares is a great way to get your products known, especially as you will be dealing with people in the right area for your business and affording them the opportunity to see your work first hand, to actually hold it and see how it works, how it is put together and just how good it is etc. You may need an introduction to be invited to exhibit if space is limited and so your former employer can really help here, but even if you do not need an introduction having one can be very valuable in helping to get you a soft landing and a good spot. Depending on the size, type and location of the fair it may or may not be an occasion at which both caterers and makers of dolls' houses will exhibit, but often the fairs for all different areas of business are run by the same companies or venues so an introduction is still very relevant and welcome.

Joining forces to create a more engaging offer
This may be as simple as creating a more attractive stand at craft fairs etc., offering to provide your previous employer with a dolls' house which can be used as a feature in their shop, or it may involve a joint offer such as complimentary (and even complementary!) foodstuffs with each dolls' house purchased etc.

Whatever feels right for the occasion, it can help to give both you and your former employer the edge over the competition.

So no matter how far apart your old and new careers are, taking pains to ensure you leave your job well can pay dividends in both the short and long term as well as providing a ready-made fall back option.

KEY THINGS TO REMEMBER

▶ *The perfect opportunity to leave your job is unlikely to magically present itself so you will need to engineer it – at the time which best suits you.*

▶ *Leave your current employment on the best possible terms to ensure a seat will always be kept warm there for you should you ever need to return.*

▶ *Your first conversation with your employer should not be about leaving, even if you have decided this is what you are going to do, but about your future.*

▶ *Capitalize on this opportunity to learn from your bosses what they most value about you in order to refine your offer once you become your own boss, and to plug any gaps in your abilities.*

▶ *Compile a list of all the people in your old company whom you really rate and make sure you stay in regular contact with them once you have left.*

▶ *Make sure you get an early heads up if anyone in your old company whom you really rate is moving on, either into another company or to become their own boss.*

▶ *Compile a database of all the people you have ever worked with, clients and potential clients (not on your employer's computer!).*

▶ *Get your employment contract reviewed by an employment lawyer.*

▶ *Ensure you have set up as many practical elements of your new business as possible before quitting your job.*

▶ *Scrutinize your old and new careers to identify all the points of convergence and create a plan to capitalize on as many as possible.*

5

What becoming your own boss actually means – and how to do it

In this chapter you will learn:
- **what is involved in being your own boss**
- **how to envisage the route**
- **how to take 'baby steps' to start with**
- **how to create the right impression**
- **about turning your passion into your job**
- **how to fine-tune your offer**

> **'The way to get started is to quit talking and begin doing.'**
>
> Walt Disney

What is involved in being your own boss?

What does it mean to become your own boss? Working your own hours, days, weeks; finishing work whenever you feel like it; picking and choosing your clients; keeping all the rewards of your efforts; standing on your own two feet and all the attendant pride that creates ... There are indeed many wonderful reasons for making the leap to becoming your own boss if you decide to quit your job or if your job decides to quit you. But these are not what becoming your own boss actually *means*, what it entails and requires in order to give it the best possible chance of succeeding. What it means is carefully thinking through all the myriad steps which you will need to take in order to have at your disposal all those things you take for granted in a 'standard' job: a defined working structure; knowing who you are working for and when, and what that work will entail; knowing that there is a support system in place in case you get stuck and need advice or fall ill and cannot work for a while; or simply need the stationery cupboard to be full all the time and all those documents typed and photocopied and left on your desk ready for tomorrow etc.

Case study

'Working for a large company I had become very used to having all the practical elements of my work needs catered for. It wasn't until I left to become my own boss that I realized the extent to which I had relied on them, and just how many there were. It's so easy to take them for granted and it requires a lot of time and effort to get them all set up in your new working life, but ultimately it's time very well spent.'

Becoming your own boss means taking charge of your working life and creating for yourself, often from scratch, the structure you think you will need in your day-to-day working life – and then rigorously testing it. Planning ahead in the early stages can save an awful lot of headaches and wasted time further down the track.

Insight
The quantity of effort you put in at this stage will be reflected in the quality of your offer when your business goes 'live'.

Envisaging the route

One of the most common mistakes people make when they decide to set up on their own for the first time is that they envisage how they want the company to look, to feel, to be defined, and with a clear vision of the big picture go marching straight into launching their new career without having given pause for thought as to how they will actually achieve this, and how the company will operate on a day-to-day basis.

Case study

'You must be prepared and think it through from every angle, the requirements and practicalities of your new working life, all the boring bits! I had thought it through very carefully, looking at each stage in turn but there were still some surprises.'

Let us look at an example. You have decided that you want to leave your current employment as an insurance salesperson and set up your own business as a photographer. After all, photography is your one true passion and all your friends and family are always telling you how good you are and, crucially, you believe in yourself, so it is the logical choice. You have thought it through, costed it as best you can plus a little extra for contingencies, and you are all set and ready to go. Except of course that you are not. Nowhere near. You have got a clear vision for your business, which is excellent, but you do not have a clear workstage structure. You have not thought through the entire process of setting up your business, in purely practical grass roots terms, envisaging all the nuts and bolts details. It is all very well deciding that you are going to launch yourself as a photographer and that you will do weddings at the weekends and studio portrait work during the week with schools' photographs at the end of term, and that you are going to call yourself 'Big Smiles

Photography' and set up in a unit on the local industrial park, but if you have not planned how you will go about finding a suitable place, whether you are going to decorate it or get someone else in to do it for you (with the attendant cost) and how you would like it to be decorated and where you will source all those bits and bobs of equipment and miscellaneous items from, how you will generate your client base (including researching what the local competition is and whether you might be better off setting up somewhere less desirable to you but with less attendant competition) and so on, then there will almost certainly be a number of unpleasant surprises which await you – most of which could and should have been avoided. So thinking through each facet of your future business, and each stage of each facet, is vitally important.

> ## Insight
>
> In some cases not carefully planning each facet of your business well in advance can quickly spell disaster and the end of being your own boss before you have properly got your feet under the table, your new career and your business dreams in tatters.

So, you have decided that you want to focus on studio portrait photography during the week and schools' photographs at the end of term, and we will assume for argument's sake that you have already established that there are local schools who might be interested in your services, for the right price, and who are not tied into long-term contracts with other photographers or franchisees of large-scale photographic enterprises. You have done some research and found that most of your studio work is likely to come from family portraits, either as family groups or of individual children or groups of children creating photos ready to be displayed on the walls of family homes by proud parents and grandparents. So far so good. You advertise locally and get a booking for one such family portrait session for 8.30 a.m. on the very first day that you will be trading. Perfect! Your studio will be decorated the previous week by a professional decorator you have employed and so it should all be looking tip-top for your first professional contract. What could possibly go wrong?

You arrive at the studio at 8.00 a.m. ready to launch your new career only to find a note from the decorator explaining that he did not have sufficient paint in the right special order colour to complete the work and so he will be back in two weeks to complete the job. In the meantime the studio looks a bit sorry for itself but at least it is serviceable; or rather it would be if it were not freezing cold, so you switch on the heater only to realize that even at its maximum output it is going to take several hours before the studio shakes off its chill – and your clients are arriving in half an hour. Not only that, but as the building starts to get a bit warmer the new paint begins to give off a strong odour, not unpleasant and certainly fresh smelling, but you know that within a very short space of time you and your clients are going to have monster headaches. Unperturbed, you set up your equipment and immediately realize that the cold and damp meeting the heat has caused the lens to fog up and you keep your fingers crossed that it will have demisted by the time your clients arrive. Except that they are already here, early and as eager as you are. You welcome them in and quickly have them arranged in an agreeable pose but the young children need something to keep them occupied, which is when you realize that you should have thought to buy some soft toys and probably some props too.

All of which pales in comparison to the oversight now dawning on you that you need to be checked and licensed by the appropriate authorities before you are allowed to work with children, a process which could take months to complete. Not only do you lose these clients, their goodwill, and the goodwill of everyone to whom they relate their disastrous experience at your hands, but you have wasted all the money you have spent in advertising your new business because by the time you are cleared to go everyone will have forgotten about you. Worse, you will have to turn away everyone who contacts you for your services over the coming months. In one fell swoop, by not having thought through all the myriad requirements of becoming your own boss, one practical step at a time, you have shot yourself in the foot to such a degree that the very existence of your new business is threatened.

'Failing to plan means planning to fail. What are your goals?'

(author unknown)

Granted it is an extreme example, but the pitfalls are all too real and really do sink a great many businesses each and every year, good businesses with sound long-term strategies and detailed business plans, simply because no one had established the day-to-day goals and needs of the business and thought through the potential obstacles along the way created by the practicalities relevant to the new business. So make sure you think through each individual stage, each separate requirement, no matter how small, and try to envisage any potential problems. For each and every item, facet and stage of your business ask yourself this simple question: if a roadblock is going to appear here to hinder progress, what is it most likely to be? What will it look like and how will it present itself? How can it be avoided? Then ask yourself what the second and third most likely roadblocks are, plus any others including the unlikely ones. Allocate a timescale to each so that if there is something which needs to be ordered months in advance it will not catch you out at the last minute.

Insight

Remember the six Ps: Proper Planning and Preparation Prevents Poor Performance.

Give yourself plenty of time to get things organized and you will be giving yourself, and your business, every chance to succeed. If you need extra motivation for doing this (and you will – it can be a painstaking, protracted and laborious process) then just bear in mind how extremely frustrating, not to mention heartbreaking it will be, and how foolish and regretful you will feel, if your quest to be your own boss fails simply because of some eminently preventable oversights.

Baby steps

Once you have everything planned in meticulous detail it is time to put it into action.

'Inaction breeds doubt and fear. Action breeds confidence and courage. If you want to conquer fear, do not sit home and think about it. Go out and get busy.'

Dale Carnegie

Hopefully you will have a budget in mind and a target for client capture and/or sales so it is a good idea at this stage to revisit these and make sure that your enthusiasm and desire to succeed have not blunted your perception of what you might realistically expect to achieve and when. There is no point in planning to become the world's number one retailer of beauty products in the next five years, or to become the world's best known and best loved photographer by Christmas, because it simply will not happen; and that is not being pessimistic or defeatist, it is simply the truth, and maintaining a healthy and realistic perspective will help to prevent you from feeling like your business is failing when it might actually be doing very well. What is more, trying to reach too high too soon can lead to disasters. One of the most common mistakes that new business owners make is allotting too much of the initial budget to advertising and marketing, putting unnecessary pressure on their business finances and risking a cash-flow problem all too soon. The reasoning is usually sound in that they are hoping to announce their arrival in a big way and get known as quickly as possible in order to begin generating income as soon as possible. The pitfall is that until the business is established there is not too much to say other than, 'We are here and this is what we do.' It is reputation that really counts and for that you need to begin trading and get references from satisfied (or hopefully ecstatic) customers and/or clients. Then as word of mouth begins to gather momentum and the good name and reputation of your business starts to spread you should back it up with an advertising and marketing campaign which really has something to shout about, full of great customer quotes about a company people at least have half a chance of having heard about.

Another common reason why people who have recently become their own boss spend too much of their initial budget on promotional materials is, quite simply, over-excitement.

Having spent months and quite possibly years dreaming of becoming their own boss and seeing their company's name in lights, the minute they see their dream becoming reality they rush headlong into commissioning a range of promotional materials (glossy pamphlets, full-colour flyers and posters, completely unnecessary – and often tacky – merchandise etc.), over-spending on marketing and advertising in their eagerness to prove to the world and to themselves that their business has arrived, that their dream is now a reality, and to gain validation as their own boss and to impress their friends and family.

Creating the right impression

In the early stages of your business you need to concentrate on creating the best possible impression with the minimum outlay and initially you will probably only need three design elements – a logo, business cards and some stationery.

LOGO

It is said that a picture speaks a thousand words, and a good logo can certainly communicate an awful lot of information about your company. It should do far more than simply make the name stand out and try to make it memorable. Your company's logo should be a reflection of your company's brands and values. One look at your logo should be sufficient to give any prospective clients a feel for what sort of company it is and for a start-up company it might well be worth investing in a logo which also communicates what your company offers. Are you offering a service? Are you a supplier? A consultant? Blue collar or white collar? Is your offer pitched at the top end, high value-high price tag, of a market into which you are offering something truly unique or are you entering an already overcrowded arena and hoping to carve a niche by doing things just a little bit differently/cheaper/better? There is, of course, a cost implication here unless you happen to be a designer and so it is something you need to weigh up carefully, but do not be tempted to cut corners and do things on the cheap. Yes, there are plenty of web-based companies who can print your cards at very competitive rates, which is excellent, but unless you have a logo with which you can present them you will end up just choosing from a limited template of pre-existing logos and nothing screams 'cheap new start-up' quite so loudly as a cookie-cutter logo.

> 'An image is not simply a trademark, a design, a slogan or an easily remembered picture. It is a studiously crafted personality profile of an individual, institution, corporation, product or service.'
>
> Daniel J. Boorstin

How much time and money you want to invest will depend largely on the type of business you are setting up (clients will expect a new advertising agency or accountancy firm to have a smarter logo than a new window cleaning company or dog walking service), but one fact is constant across the board – it really is worth investing in a bespoke logo. Then, depending on what sort of company you are setting up, you might be ready to get your business cards printed and start getting the word out. If this is the case it is probably not going to be worth getting a designer involved to create the layout for your cards – this is a service which a great many web-based printing companies offer free of charge if you get them to print your cards. They will also offer to save the template so that you can get more printed at any time which is perfect – they make sure they will get your repeat business and you do not have to spend time and energy on the hassle of redesigning your cards each time. It also keeps initial capital outlay to a minimum since you need only order the quantity of cards you think you are likely to need to get up and running; a six-month supply is probably about right for most businesses. It is worth bearing in mind that this quantity is likely to be considerably more than you will require for the same period later in your business' life, particularly if you are intending to hand them out as cost-effective one-to-one advertising, so bump up the volume accordingly.

BUSINESS CARDS AND STATIONERY

Clients will receive hundreds of business cards in any given year. Likewise letters with fancy letterheads. So how do you make sure yours stand out from the crowd and rise to the top of the pile? How do you make sure yours are the cream of the crop without them costing you the earth? We have already looked at the need for good logos, so hopefully you will have that as a good starting point. Depending on your type of business, creating business cards and stationery may be as simple as positioning your logo on a standard letterhead and adding any necessary details such as company name and address, company number, VAT registration number, standard payment terms etc. If, on the other hand, you are creating the sort of business where a whole raft of stationery is in order, or simply one where a great logo sat on a bog standard business card won't cut the mustard, then you need to allocate sufficient funds to getting a designer on board. It is worth spending the time and effort required to find the right designer for you and your business, someone with a good portfolio of work of the ilk you have got in mind for your business, and preferably a one-person outfit who will not only very likely be cheaper than an established design agency but who will also better understand the position you are in and what you need their design to achieve (after all, they were in the same boat too).

Thankfully there are some great freelance designers only too happy to engage in this sort of work and finding the right one for you should not be too much of a problem, but do make sure you ask to see some of their recent work before committing yourself to them since you might be asked to pay some money up front. This is not unreasonable on their part since they will be investing time in creating bespoke designs for your company and if you later decide to go with someone else they could be left holding the baby. So choose carefully, be prepared to pay some money up front, and then give them a really clear brief. It need not be long-winded and ultra detailed in terms of how you would like the finished product to look (in fact it is usually best if it is not – it is called a 'brief' for a reason); just make sure that they understand the type of company you are creating, your target market for receivership of the stationery, and any brand values you want to communicate. A good brief might look something like this:

Company name: Crystal Clear Communications

What we do: Crystal Clear Communications is a copywriting agency specializing in advertising copy, above and below the line

What we want to achieve:

Ideally the logo will:

▶ *communicate modernity and that the company is a powerhouse of creativity, taking a fresh and dynamic approach to conventional copywriting challenges*
▶ *feel 'edgy', urban, and a little bit quirky*

Ideally the logo will not:

▶ *have anything obviously to do with words or writing*
▶ *appear 'old school'*

Of course it is easy to get carried away here – you have just decided to set up your own company and there is an overwhelming urge to make it as flash as possible and splash out on an expensive designer logo and the most expensive business cards printed on the thickest card or perhaps made of see-through plastic, as well as all manner of stationery you will probably never need to use. So think carefully through your business needs and be realistic and honest enough to filter out your own desires for anything which will make you feel good but which is unnecessary for your business.

Turning your passion into your job

Have you ever found yourself ruing the long hours you have to spend at work, yearning for the weekends when you can devote some quality time to pursuing your hobby? And have you found yourself dreaming of the workplace utopia that getting paid to carry out your hobby, allowing you to quit work altogether, would constitute? The truth is that a great many people dream this dream every day, but precious few ever do anything about it. One of the main reasons for this is that while it would constitute the best of all worlds, people are reluctant to believe that it could actually work, or more precisely that it could actually work for them. If you find yourself in this position and you have determined that you are the sort of person who could thrive being your own boss, then it is time to do a little research and honestly answer some tough questions to ascertain whether or not your hobby can support you and you really can turn your passion into your full-time occupation.

Insight

Remember that you do not have to make the leap to becoming your own boss and changing your career in one go. In the first instance it may be prudent to become your own boss in a familiar field to the one in which you have been gainfully employed, gradually making the transition to setting up a business focused on your hobby over a period of time once you have become used to being your own boss.

YOUR HOBBY'S EARNING POTENTIAL

Is your hobby something at which you can foresee yourself earning
enough money to live on? Indeed, is it something for which you are
realistically likely to get paid at all? It is all very well dreaming of
making money from carrying out your hobby, but how thoroughly
have you tested its true market potential? Do you provide a service
people require and will be willing to pay for? Do you create a
product people will want to buy? Have you really put your offer
to the test or are you basing your judgement solely on the positive
reactions of family and friends (and remember, family and friends
can nearly always be guaranteed to be positive!). Before taking
the leap to turning your passion into your job, you need to ensure
there is a marketplace sufficient to support it, and not just for the
short term. Rigorous research is called for, and plenty of it. The
internet provides invaluable access to all sorts of sites which will
help you to draw a clear picture of the market opportunities for
your hobby and its true market potential. Also make sure you
research your local area if your offer is to provide something close
to home to make sure it is not already saturated. Ask yourself the
following questions:

- *Is there definitely a need for my offer?*
- *Is there room in the marketplace (local or other)?*
- *Am I providing/creating anything unique?*
- *How frequently is my offer likely to be taken up?*
- *How much will I be able to charge?*
- *Is my offer sustainable for the mid or long term?*

The last point is particularly important if you are expecting this
work life step-change to be workable for the foreseeable future.
There is no point heading into it if you know that two years
down the line the work is likely to dry up. Be honest with yourself –
is your offer based on a fleeting fashion or temporary trend,
something which is all the rage now but which might drop off the
radar in a year or two? Are you hoping to cash in on a fad? If so,
is the offer transmutable to take advantage of the next craze, or

are you confident you will have made sufficient money by then not to have to worry? Is your offer occasion based? (It's all very well if you can make considerable money on your first day but if those days are few and far between you might well come unstuck. Beware all Coronation flag sellers!).

YOUR EXPECTATIONS

Having established a realistic idea of your hobby's earning potential it is time for some soul-searching: how much – or rather how little – money would you be willing to live on? There is a very realistic chance that no matter how good your product or service is and no matter how good you are at providing it, it is not going to generate the sort of income you have been used to in your paid employ, at least not at first. So you need to be realistic about the amount of money you would be willing to come down to as a living wage, and for how long. In the first instance you will need to ensure that you will at least be bringing in sufficient funds to cover your outgoings, not on a business footing (which should be taken as read) but on a personal level – paying the mortgage, bills, council tax and the myriad other financial commitments you may have. Any surplus may then be regarded as disposable income – if there is any surplus, that is. It is amazing how many people decide to jump ship and rely on their erstwhile hobby to provide their income without properly understanding the economics and are then amazed to find themselves struggling to make ends meet. A rigorous audit at this stage might throw up some painful truths, or even dash your hopes entirely, but it will be far more painful to give up your income stream only to then realize the hard way that you have made a big mistake. So, be brutally honest about where you can and will be happy to tighten your belt, remembering it may have to be for the medium to long term; this way if you do decide to take the plunge you will have the reassurance that you are going into it with your eyes open and that you have done everything possible to ensure there will be as few nasty surprises as possible awaiting you.

Fine-tuning your offer

If you have decided that everything stacks up financially, then there is one more task you will need to complete in order to get all your ducks in a row, namely fine-tuning your offer. This is where a great many people come unstuck for one simple reason – it often means moving away from what you really want to do, which was the whole reason for leaving your job to do it in the first place. Let us take an example. Jean worked as a school administration officer for more than 20 years, during which time she pursued her passion for cross-stitch, completing dozens of designs from simple, small pictures to large elaborate scenes, but all featuring one common theme – her other passion, cats. Encouraged by friends and family she took early retirement to concentrate on her cross-stitch with a view to capitalizing on the uptake of the internet to showcase her work and secure sales. It quickly became apparent, however, that there was a limited market for cross-stitch pictures of cats and feline-inspired scenes; the real market was in accepting commissions for bespoke designs often incorporating a person's name or a special date etc. Unfortunately hardly any of these included pictures of cats! Moreover, the price Jean found she could charge did not increase *pro rata* with the increased size of larger works – in fact a very small piece which she could complete in an afternoon would fetch about a quarter of the price of that she could charge for the largest pieces, which could take several weeks. Therefore, although Jean's passion was for the larger pieces, with designs prominently featuring cats, the market opportunity was obvious – bespoke commissions of small, usually cat-free pieces. At this point she had a clear choice to make – stick to her real passion, the thing she had been doing when she took early retirement and dreamed of continuing as a career, or switch to the type of cross-stitch that people wanted to buy and were willing to pay for. In other words, continue to view the cross-stitch as a hobby or start to think of it as a business and treat it as a job.

Case study

'I weighed up all the options available to me and after discussing it with family and friends I had a pretty clear idea of the realities of the situation so looking back I can't really justify my decision to concentrate on the large designs of cats instead of the small individually commissioned and unique pieces which I knew was where the money lay. I think if I am completely honest it was probably for two reasons. Firstly, this is what I had spent countless hours, days, years, dreaming of doing while I was still at work. Secondly, since these are my true love I felt that not concentrating on them was in some bizarre way selling out. Every time I thought about it I knew that it wasn't the sensible decision and my husband kept reminding me that I wasn't making a sensible business decision but I felt it was what I had to do and I knew that if I didn't I would spend all the time feeling guilty! It only took me three months however to realize my mistake and thankfully I now have a thriving business accepting commissions for small bespoke cross-stitch pieces.'

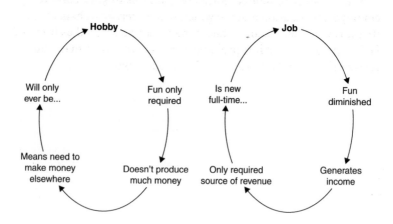

Hobby
- Will only ever be...
- Fun only required
- Doesn't produce much money
- Means need to make money elsewhere

Job
- Is new full-time...
- Fun diminished
- Generates income
- Only required source of revenue

If you are serious about wanting to turn your passion into your job then you may well have to accept that there will need to be compromises along the way. But they do not necessarily have to be earth-shattering; indeed if they are then something has gone very wrong along the way because your new job is in danger of becoming everything your old job was and there will be no reason left for making the switch! Worse still, you will no longer have any of the benefits that you had whilst working for your previous employer.

Insight

Two common mindset traps to avoid:

▶ *people will readily pay you to pursue your passion exactly as you have always dreamed*
▶ *if you cannot pursue your passion exactly as you would like to then you might as well not bother at all.*

Draw a clear picture for yourself of what your new job would look like – not the idealized version you have probably been nursing for years where you can do exactly what pleases you and get paid lots of money for your troubles, but the realistic version, warts and all, of what you will need to be doing every day in order to make your new career profitable. Then compare this to your current employment situation and see which you prefer. The chances are that it is the new job, and while it might not be as good as it would be in a perfect world it is probably significantly better than your present situation. Crucially, it is realistic and workable.

KEY THINGS TO REMEMBER

▶ *In addition to having a clear long-term goal for your business you will need to think through the myriad practicalities which will need to be undertaken to ensure you are not caught out by any unexpected roadblocks.*

▶ *Not allowing yourself plenty of time to properly think through every facet of the needs of your business on a day-by-day, week-by-week, month-by-month, year-by-year basis can spell disaster for your new business before it is even properly launched.*

▶ *Spend only as much as you really need to on promotional materials – avoid the temptation to commission too much too soon in your enthusiasm for your new business.*

▶ *Your hobby may not translate directly into a viable business.*

▶ *Be clear how much of the enjoyment you get from your hobby you will need to sacrifice if it becomes your business, and how much you are willing to sacrifice.*

▶ *Ensure you have a realistic understanding of the amount of money your hobby is likely to generate as a business, and a realistic expectation of the sort of lifestyle to which you might be limited.*

▶ *Make sure you have a crystal clear vision of how your hobby will become your career, ensuring that it is realistic and workable, and set yourself a timeframe for achieving this so that you can monitor your progress and measure your success.*

6

Setting up your solo work life

In this chapter you will learn:
- *about the best place for you to work*
- *about sharing, renting or buying an office*
- *about the pros and cons of working from home*

Where to work?

The exact requirements of your working environment will of course differ from person to person according to the type of work you intend to pursue and there is not room in this book – there is not room in *any* book – to detail them all. If you intend to carve out a career in sculpting this will obviously require a different working environment to that required for car maintenance or a large-scale bakery and so on and so on. What is common to these types of businesses is that they require premises uniquely suited to a very specific set of requirements, and if you intend to become your own boss in such a field then the chances are you will know what these should be like. Far more difficult is the choice for the solo office worker or small-scale manufacturer, as so many more options are open to you and you will need to think through what feels right for you as well as what looks right for your business. Should you opt to work from home or rent an office space? Should you purchase an office space? Is it preferable to work alongside other likeminded people, albeit completely independent of them, or is it better to have your own secluded space? While finding the right business premises clearly is not as important as defining the right business opportunity, it should nevertheless be high on your list of priorities, not least because it is going to help shape the way you feel about your new venture, and at a time of great uncertainty and change in your working life this is very important. The positive impact of working in an inspiring environment is difficult to overstate – you will feel energized and excited every time you come to work. Equally, just settling for somewhere which is far from perfect but which you reckon will probably be okay is a recipe for disaster, or at the very least will handicap the potential of your business. If you cannot find anything that is exactly right then you might need to be prepared to make some alterations and improvements yourself.

> **'Strive for perfection in everything you do. Take the best that exists and make it better. If it does not exist, invent it. Accept nothing which is nearly right or good enough.'**
>
> Sir Frederick Henry Royce

Look at it this way – if you have spent endless hours developing business plans and marketing strategies, invested time and money in establishing your new company's identity, made huge efforts setting up your first piece of work and perhaps securing funding, does it not make sense to spend the time required to find the right home for your business? After all, you will be spending an awful lot of time there and it is where your new fledgling business, and your dreams, will either take off or wither and die.

Sharing an office

For many people one of the great benefits of becoming their own boss is that it enables them to work from home, or at least to be based there. The advantages are clear: office space is free of charge, the commute is non-existent, and all the advantages of home are right there for the taking. The trouble is, so are all the disadvantages: distractions are present in many different forms throughout the house; self-motivation can often be most difficult when you are completely alone and the isolation, while great for concentration, can prove to be very lonely. Here is a checklist of some of the major points you will need to consider before making your decision:

▶ *Are you willing to pay to rent space in a shared office? Will the potential benefits outweigh the cost, e.g. will the extra motivation enable you to generate more work? How much extra revenue is it likely to help you to bring in (over and above any that you would have earned anyway working from home)? By how much will this outweigh the extra costs incurred, including the commute, parking, ordering pizza into the office on those days when you simply have to work late etc.?*

▶ *Is the lack of a commute a good or a bad thing? Will you devote the extra time to securing and completing additional profitable work? Would a commute help you to separate your home life from your work life and provide a necessary transition, both physically so that you know you have completed a journey and 'arrived at work' and mentally so you feel you are now at work, having had time to make the transition and get your head into gear and into work mode?*

▶ *Will working in a dedicated space help you to focus more effectively and boost your profitability?*

▶ *Will having other people around you during your working day help to motivate you or just provide unwanted distractions? (Bear in mind that they will not necessarily, or even likely, be involved in the same line of work as you.)*

▶ *Will you be provided with all the resources you need to work effectively? For example, are printers provided for clients' use, and are there a sufficient number and of the required quality? Is there an additional charge for use of these facilities over and above the standard rental fee? Is there a suitable internet connection? Are telephone lines and fax facilities provided? Are these dedicated to each workstation or communal? Is there provision of decent tea and coffee?!*

▶ *Are there any networking possibilities provided by renting a shared office space, even if there is no one else in the office in the same line of work as you? For example, one of the desks might be rented by a designer who can give you a preferential rate on designing your company logo and stationery.*

▶ *Will you be provided with your own desk or workstation or does everyone in the office hot desk? Which suits you best?*

▶ *Is there space you can use for meetings? If you need to invite clients to meetings then not having to shop around to find a suitable venue to hire can save you both time and money (do not ever make the mistake of inviting them to your office at home!).*

▶ *How long is the rental agreement? Can you opt out early without incurring a heavy penalty if you discover that it is not working for you?*

Individual business needs and thus the options available will vary markedly from one person to the next (and from one business to the next), so make a list of all the pros and cons specific to your business, your needs and, crucially, your personality and see whether renting a space in a shared office is right for you. If you think that it is, there are plenty of companies who will be more than happy to assist you in finding a suitable venue, but treat it much as you would treat purchasing a new house. Do not be in a hurry to make your decision, do not believe all the sales pitches you are given by people who stand to make commission from your commitment, and make sure you visit several places before settling on one.

Renting an office

If having a dedicated place of work is important to you but the idea of sharing an office leaves you cold then renting your own dedicated office could be the answer. It is more costly so you will need to be very clear about the perceived benefits and regularly review the situation to see if it is matching up to what you had envisaged. You will need to find a way to equate the cost with the additional value the space gives you and your business and this will be different for each business and indeed for each individual.

Again, ensure that the terms of the lease fit with your plans, and take your time to ensure that the office space is just right for your needs. Selecting the right environment is crucial to the successful running of your new business.

Insight

Your search for suitable business premises will be a lot easier, and quicker, if you ensure you have thought through your business needs carefully and structured a list of clear objectives and defined criteria before setting out.

If you do decide to rent an office space then selecting the appropriate one will be crucial to your business success; working in the best possible environment for you will help to put you in the right frame of mind and provide a daily fillip to your working life, and it can also help you to grow your business by providing the right corporate image, offering suitable meeting space etc. Listed below are some of the more common pointers of which you will need to be aware when selecting your new premises for rental:

▶ *What is your budget? Do not forget to include any upfront deposit you might need to put down, monthly or annual service charges you may need to pay (and whether these are payable in advance or in arrears), and any alterations or decorative improvements you may wish to implement.*
▶ *Serviced or unserviced offices? The latter are of course almost always cheaper but you will need to be aware of all the additional costs you might incur such as heating, lighting, insurance etc. Is it worth paying the premium for the convenience of serviced offices?*
▶ *Where do you want to be situated? Offices in rural locations, rundown areas of a city, those without convenient transport links or situated a long way from amenities will often command a lower rental but will this be at the cost of your business? Is your new office for your use only, somewhere to go so that you do not have to work at home, or is it intended to be a location to which you can invite visitors? If so, will they be able to find you quickly and easily? Will they even be*

bothered to try? Do you hope to attract business from passers-by? Do large-scale deliveries preclude renting offices at the end of an unmade road? And so on.

▶ *Will you have visitors to your premises and if so how important to you and your business is your corporate image? For example, if you are setting up as an accountant will it matter if your new offices are located above a bingo hall?*

▶ *How large does your office need to be? Do you simply need a desk in the corner of a room or will you be employing someone to help you from day one? (A good rule of thumb is to allow 80 ft^2 [7.5 m^2] per person.) Will you need to accommodate visitors, customers, suppliers etc.?*

▶ *Do the offices cater for the needs of disabled employees, visitors etc.?*

▶ *Will your new office space afford you the degree of privacy you desire for your business, or do you prefer the feel of being in the middle of a busy office environment?*

▶ *How good (and how important to you and your business) are the communal facilities, e.g. toilets, meeting rooms, kitchen etc.?*

▶ *How good is the IT infrastructure? Will you need to invest in upgrading any systems? How much is this likely to cost?*

▶ *For how long do you envisage renting the office space? Will it be appropriate to your needs in the medium to long term? What are the terms of the rental agreement (for example, can you leave after a short period of notice or are you tied in for several years?). Does the space match your long-term business plan and forecast? Are there other areas of the building into which you could move your business as it grows or would an expanding business require a complete relocation?*

Buying an office

Another option open to you is to purchase your own office space. Obviously the costs, and particularly the upfront costs, are significant when compared with renting so you should only take this step if you are as certain as you can be that your business will be successful and that you are in it for the long term. Many of the points listed above are also relevant when buying an office, but you need to be mindful of the fact that if after a period of time you realize you have made a mistake (in the location of your office, its facilities, its long-term potential for an expanding business etc.) then there is no handy end of contract period to act as a convenient get-out clause. Instead you will be lumbered with all the hassles, and costs, of selling your office and buying – or renting – somewhere else.

If you are not 100 per cent certain that buying an office is the right course of action for you, at this juncture a safer and more sensible option might be to rent an office space on a short-term contract to see how it works out. This will allow you to get the feel of the set-up and scope out the lie of the land for your new business before committing it, and yourself, to something much longer term and much more costly.

Insight

If possible include an opt-out clause in your rental so that if the trial proves successful you can make the move to purchasing your premises that much earlier.

Listed below are some of the more common pointers of which you will need to be aware when selecting your new premises for purchase:

▶ *You are signing up for a long-term commitment.*
▶ *If you need a mortgage, most lenders will require a substantial deposit.*
▶ *The interest rate on your mortgage may well vary over time making it more difficult to budget accurately.*
▶ *Your premises will be subject to fluctuations in the property market.*
▶ *If the value of your property increases you may well be liable to Capital Gains Tax when you come to sell.*
▶ *You will be responsible for the upkeep of your office, inside and out.*

Working from home

To most people this seems like the obvious and the best choice. Everything you require will be to hand and you will be able to dispense with a miserable commute, allowing you to spend that time working instead. What is more, because you will be based at home you will have all the comforts of home to enjoy all day and every day. What could possibly be better than that?

The inconvenient truth however is that there are significant downsides to working from home. While everything you require may be to hand they will be accompanied by myriad distractions as you battle to keep your home life and work life separate. You may have done away with the daily commute, but with it you will lose an excellent opportunity to mentally shake off your home life with all its attendant joys, worries, expectations and distractions and prepare yourself for the working day ahead. If you are going to work from home, is there a dedicated space you can use as your office?

Case study

'I think most people who work at home need to be able to flick an imaginary switch in their head so that they go into business mode each day. Having a proper office or workshop helps to do that.'

As for home comforts being permanently on tap, anyone who has become their own boss and opted to work from home will know that this is very much a double-edged sword. Working from home might well prove to be your best option, and it will almost certainly be the cheapest one, but it is not without risks. The following chapters will help to ensure your eyes are wide open to the realities of the situation if you take the leap not only to becoming your own boss but to doing so from your own home.

KEY THINGS TO REMEMBER

▶ *Weigh up the pros and cons of working from home versus renting an office space versus purchasing an office.*

▶ *If you think renting or purchasing an office space is the best option make sure you visit several before settling on one, and do not believe all the sales pitches you are given!*

▶ *Offices with lower rental fees usually entail compromises of one sort or another (accessibility, look and feel, equipment provided etc.) and working out what is important to you and your business is crucial to securing an appropriate venue.*

▶ *Ensure any potential business premises has, or has the potential to acquire, everything your business needs, e.g. IT infrastructure, disabled access, privacy, accessibility to visitors etc.*

▶ *Be clear about your future business plans to ensure any space you rent or buy has the potential to accommodate your business as it expands.*

▶ *If you intend to purchase an office, consider renting one for a short period beforehand in order to test the water and make sure that this type of set-up really works for you.*

▶ *Working from home might seem to be the obvious solution but it is not without risks – for you and for your family; ensure you are aware of these before committing yourself to this course of action.*

7

Effective home working

In this chapter you will learn:
- *how to use your home as your office*
- *how to separate your work life from your home life in terms of time and space*
- *how to create the right working environment and maximize efficiency in your workspace*

Using your home as your office

As we have already seen in the previous chapter, there can be significant downsides to using your home as your office, both for you and for your family; but there can be significant upsides too. Get the balance right and you may well find yourself in the enviable position of having more time to spend with your family and friends as well as being able to devote more time to your business. With any luck you should be able to create your *ideal* working environment and, provided you are conscious of the many potential pitfalls to working from home, you should be able to successfully navigate around them. If working from home means denying your family access to one room and to you while you are 'at work', then this will need to be carefully managed, but provided you do so, and provided that anyone with whom you share your home (and thus, now, your working environment) is supportive of your venture, there is no reason why you should not be able to make the transition to becoming your own boss while simultaneously making the transition to working from home.

'I have an office in my home, which we have recently made much more comfortable and efficient. We should have done that sooner. Firstly you need to be efficient – not mixing business and domestic material, etc. Secondly you need to have a room which does not feel too homely, otherwise you'll be prone to slips of discipline. Never, ever work in earshot of a television!'

Achieving the best work/life balance

Perhaps the single biggest challenge any home-alone worker faces is the juggling of home life and work life given that, by definition, these occupy the same space. It is therefore vitally important that you develop strategies to separate them – both for you and for anyone who lives with you.

Insight

Killing your business with kindness: well-meaning family and friends can be the single biggest threat to your business – bar none.

Working at home can certainly take some getting used to. It is all too easy to underestimate the skills and determination required. The constant temptation to become side-tracked by home life, coupled with the capacity for never-ending interruptions from family who think that as you are at home you are not working, can have a serious negative impact on your business unless it is carefully managed. On the other hand it is very easy to go too far the other way, particularly in the early stages of becoming your own boss, and the worry of allowing your home life to merge with your work life detrimentally might cause you to shut out your family completely – and needlessly. So how do you achieve the optimum work/life balance?

Case study

'Since I went solo, I have never worked over the weekend (other than leaving on Sunday evening for a flight). In big corporate life, I used to work one day every weekend. Now I am my own boss I take a day out to drive my boat every two weeks (on average). I also take eight weeks holiday a year. What I love is that I can choose what balance I want between work and life.'

The crucial task facing everyone as soon as they are their own boss and can work their own hours in any configuration that pleases them is to work out a pattern which enables you to balance your work life with your non-work life to the best effect not only for you, but for your business and your family too. You will enjoy a great degree of flexibility in your work life, and this should also be carried over into your home life. There are so many ways in which you could try to find the perfect balance, but for most people it is a case of trial and error until they get it right. Remember to review the situation frequently and to discuss it with any relevant parties to make sure that it is working to the benefit of everyone involved.

Case study

'If I wanted to I could work half as much and have double the time with my family, but earn half as much. Alternatively I could work as hard as I used to in my previous job and earn loads more, but I have found the balance that works for me and I focus on maintaining it. It's not a fixed thing – you have to work at the balance every day. But you learn how to flex it as you go along ...'

If you find that for some reason or another you are not getting the balance right and that your home life or your work life is suffering as a result, then you will need to re-examine the structure you have defined and try to pinpoint how and where it is not working. It should be relatively straightforward to determine which element of your life is too dominant and which is suffering, but creating harmony in the yin and yang of your work life/home life balance can be very challenging. However, if you managed it while you were gainfully employed then it is reasonable to assume that you should be able to manage it now that you are your own boss. Indeed you should be able to establish a superior balance; this is after all one of the benefits to becoming your own boss. If you are struggling, then rest assured that you are not alone; a great many soloists find that this is one area which seems to be particularly problematic. One of the reasons for this is that now that you no longer have the framework of a paid job where the workday and workplace structure was immovable, you need to set your own boundaries, boundaries which need to be negotiated with other members of your household whose priorities may well differ from yours! However, if you approach the challenge in a methodical manner you should find that you can make it work to the benefit of all concerned:

- ▶ *Ascertain the optimum work/life balance for you, your family, and the needs of your business.*
- ▶ *Determine which area is taking too much of the share, and to what degree.*
- ▶ *Try to identify any patterns which are causing problems in creating the desired work/life balance and establish the reasons for this.*
- ▶ *With all appropriate parties, create an action plan to remedy the imbalance.*
- ▶ *Put the plan into action and monitor the situation carefully. Be prepared to adjust as necessary.*

One word of caution – it is very easy to allow your work life to take too much precedence in your life, even if it is only allocated an appropriate share of your time. This is because your work can unbalance your home life in a different way – mentally – by never switching off. So it is very important to ensure that when you are working you focus on your work, and when you are not working you focus on letting go.

Home life versus work life – separation and synergy

Case study

'I get a sense of excitement from my work ... However, there are other things that are more important such as my family, friends, life experiences ... I therefore try to balance things out. I may spend a month focused on my projects and the next month I spend more time with the people I care for, doing things like exploring with the kids, spending time with them doing what they enjoy. There is no rule, I am flexible and I have to be flexible. One thing I have learned is to relinquish some control and have people work for me to do some of the time consuming things I don't enjoy. This has freed up a lot of my time.'

Unless you live alone, you may well find that a great portion of your time will be eroded by well-meaning visitors; partners offering a cup of coffee which segues neatly into a 20-minute discussion about domestic affairs, or the children who descend like a flock of gorgeous time-stealing treasures, or the family pooch, or ... you get the idea. And it's a real concern for every home-alone worker when they are not home alone because every valuable minute taken up with domestic issues is time stolen from the paid work you should be getting on with. To put it into perspective, try to imagine working for a large multi-national and having your partner arriving at your desk to discuss domestic issues several times each day, then throw into the mix your children, friends, dog etc. invading your office and demanding your attention ... and now try to imagine your colleagues' response – and your boss's reaction. Putting yourself mentally back into the wage-slave harness is a good way of seeing whether or not what is going on in your workspace is acceptable on a business footing.

Case study

'I work in a room in the house dedicated as an office space. I had done this for my previous job so I am used to it. It is off the kitchen which works well. The family keep out unless they need to nick paper or scissors! My laptop is out of bounds to anyone but me. It is important that these boundaries are set up from the start.'

Of course allowing, and even creating, flexibility in your work/life balance is one of the bonuses of working from home but it needs to be carefully managed. So how do you achieve the right balance without either compromising your business efficiency or alienating your family? And are you being fair to them if you impose contrived boundaries? You are, after all, physically right there in their home, a permanent presence and a constant temptation.

Time and space

TIME

Short of soundproofing your workspace and hermetically sealing yourself inside there is really only one viable solution – you need to ring-fence your time.

'The biggest challenge for me is managing my time with my family. Two of my children (aged five and seven) are at school and we also have a baby. My wife is a full-time mother and so the temptation for me to go downstairs and see them all the time is very great. Also, knowing when the children are home from school and knowing that I need to keep working is very hard, but of course it's even harder for them because they want me to play with them. Eventually we made some ground rules about when it was okay to disturb me and I became very strict with myself about when it was okay for me to disturb them! It seems odd making these boundaries in your own home, with your own family, but I think it would be impossible for me to work from home if we didn't have them.'

So, agree simple rules with family members about when it is okay to disturb you and when it is not – and decide upon some firm boundaries for yourself. You might, for instance, ensure you always take a break for half an hour when the kids get home from school and build this into your work schedule (after all, you would have taken a break at some point mid-afternoon anyway wouldn't you?), but make sure it is understood by one and all that after your break you will not reappear until dinner time. This gives everyone access to you (and you to them) without any encroachment on your work time. Taking breaks when other people are around also means you are less likely to become a recluse and start talking to the pot plant. Socializing is one of the definite upsides to being in paid employment, but it does not mean it has to be a downside to home-alone working. Just how rigid you make the times of your breaks and how keenly you enforce the rule that you are not to be disturbed depends largely on your ability to manage the situation without compromising the needs of your business or your family, but most home-alone workers find that clear boundaries not only make it easier for them to achieve the desired amount of daily work time, but easier too on the other members of the household since everyone knows exactly where they stand.

Case study

'... you have to be able not to be endlessly side-tracked by home-life or endlessly interrupted by your family who think that as you are at home, you are fair game to chat to, ask a favour of or "can you just mind the kids whilst I pop to the shops/have a nap/get my hair cut ..."'

The other advantage is that just as it prevents other people from encroaching on your work time, so equally it shields you from the temptation to spend time with them and to take more and more frequent, and longer and longer breaks. Overtly ring-fencing your time really is to the benefit of everyone.

Insight
Company is important. But so is your Company.

SPACE

Since by definition every home-alone worker works from home, it is vitally important to establish a clear demarcation between your office (working) space and your home (life) space. Creating a clear and unambiguous physical definition of your workspace is crucial to putting yourself in the right frame of mind – entering your workspace should automatically put you mentally into 'work mode'. If you are fortunate enough to have one room in your house which you can convert into an office then it should be relatively simple; if your workspace needs to double as part of your life space it can be a lot more tricky. Either way you may need to establish some ground rules with the other members of your household.

Insight

To ring-fence your time, try adopting a 'closed office door' policy.

Creating boundaries is key to safeguarding your productivity. Designating your office as off limits whenever the door is shut is a great way to achieve this, and while you may feel it is not particularly social to ban all your family members completely from one room in the house (which is, after all, their home too) it is important to have a sanctuary in which you can focus 100 per cent on your work. Just because you are in the house does not mean you are not at work and it is a good idea to get everyone on board with this as early as possible.

Quite simply, when the door to your office is open, it is open house – but as soon as you are in the office and the door is shut then you are at the office and will not be home until the door is opened. Do not disturb!

Insight

Hang a 'Do Not Disturb' sign on your office door!

Creating the right environment

It is important that your office should look and feel like a workspace. Not only does this mean that it will not feel like you are denying your family members or housemates a room they would want to be in, but it also helps to create the workspace/homespace boundary for you, propelling you into work mode the moment you cross the threshold. From a carefully placed bowl of potpourri to the installation of a grand master, from the positioning of an imposing desk to the introduction of creative-thinking beanbags, or from arranging your furniture to maximize light and space to going the whole feng shui hog and letting loose the professionals, creating a working environment that works for you is all important in the quest to maximize your working efficiency.

Case study

'I have turned the spare room into an office. After the first year of being literally in the spare room, perched on the bed and using a dressing table as my desk, I decided to create a real office. It works very well. I have a glass door, nice chairs and a huge desk. It looks and feels like my very own office. Not the product of some cost-conscious corporate "furnisher", nor a ludicrous glass and metal "designer" office that looks like a set from some tacky soap opera. It's mine and I feel very comfortable in it.'

How exactly you achieve this will depend upon a number of factors, but unless you have several million pounds to spend on fine art or a predilection for over-perfumed wood shavings the following may provide a few useful pointers:

▶ *Turn any permanent fixtures into practical office furniture (e.g. fixed wardrobes into store cupboards).*
▶ *Decorate your office in neutral tones – just take your cue from any large multi-national.*
▶ *Choose a room with a plain outlook (e.g. not onto the back garden where your kids will be playing much of the time).*
▶ *Avoid furniture which doubles for domestic duties (e.g. a sofa for those 'creative thinking' moments which converts neatly into a bed for guests, thereby converting your office into the spare bedroom and denying you any* bona fide *workspace every time you have visitors).*
▶ *Go mad on shelving – nothing makes you feel like you have arrived at work like the sight of business books and box files.*
▶ *Invest in filing cabinets – this will help to keep your desk uncluttered as well as ensuring all your vital documents are always readily to hand.*
▶ *Install lots of lights (a well-lit office makes it easier and less tiring to concentrate for long periods – you never saw a dim office in a multi-national).*
▶ *Fix blinds instead of curtains.*
▶ *Keep artwork, ornaments and nick-nacks to a minimum – if they would look out of place in the offices of a standard large multi-national, then get them out of yours.*

Insight

Creating an optimal working environment is one of the most important things you can do, but strangely it is one of the aspects of becoming your own boss which is often overlooked. Do not underestimate the importance of creating a working environment which puts you in the right frame of mind from day one, firmly putting you into work mode every time you arrive at your workspace.

Maximizing efficiency in your workspace

It is important to create an environment which suits and reflects your taste and working style, whatever these might be. If you work most effectively in a clean and tidy workspace, uncluttered and functional, then that is how your office should be. If, however, you genuinely find you are more productive in a messy environment, things flung to the four corners of the room, then that is what you should create; but be honest with yourself – do not fall into the trap of convincing yourself that you work best in a state of perpetual organized chaos just so you have an excuse to never tidy!

'To thine own self be true'

William Shakespeare

How many times have you heard people say things like:

▶ *'It may look untidy to everyone else but I know exactly where everything is.'*
▶ *'I know it's a bit of a mess but that's how I work best'?*

And how many times has that person been you? The fact is that while most of us do not keep our workspace as tidy as we should (as tidy as someone else would keep it for us if we were still in someone else's gainful employ), we always feel a sense of relief, of renaissance even, each time we do get around to the big tidy – getting up to date with the filing, with the company accounts, cleaning the office and putting away everything which can be put away and neatening anything which cannot, sorting paperwork into logical piles for quick and easy recovery and so on. And every time we think the same thought: 'That's better! Right, I definitely won't leave it so long next time ...'

Because the truth is that for 99 per cent of us a tidy and well organized work space will allow us to concentrate better, to focus our energies more accurately and to increase productivity overall.

So, when creating and maintaining your working environment, be honest about your needs.

> **'You are a product of your environment. So choose the environment that will best develop you toward your objective. Analyse your life in terms of its environment. Are the things around you helping you toward success – or are they holding you back?'**
>
> W. Clement Stone

Of course, all this assumes that you have a spare room which you can devote exclusively to being your office. But what happens if you have *no choice* but to have it double as a spare bedroom? What happens if it needs to double as *your* bedroom? This is the reality of the situation for many home-alone workers, particularly in the early days of quitting their job and becoming their own boss, and while your business aspirations may well be to have a dedicated office space in the not-too-distant future, your only viable option in the very short term might well be to make do with what you have got. After all, the expense of setting up your own business can be fairly steep and one of the key cost-savings to be enjoyed is in using your home as your work space – and if you are not lucky enough to have a spare room which can be converted into an office then doubling up on one of the rooms is the only alternative. Whether you opt for your office to double with your bedroom, living room, hallway, or even the summer house or garden shed, is going to depend largely on the demands of your non-business life (and the lives of anyone else sharing your home) but one thing remains constant: although physically needs must dictate that your office space co-habits with one of your living spaces, to all intents and purposes they should remain separate. It can be problematic enough that your workstation is in your house, but if your work space is allowed to blend with your living space and your home becomes your office then your all-important means of feeling like you have left home and arrived at work each day will quickly evaporate.

Of course, there is always an exception which proves the rule and a few (very few) home-alone workers do decide to buck the trend, go completely against received wisdom and allow their working and life spaces to merge. But while this might sound great, be warned – most people find it completely impossible to implement successfully. The upside is that, should inspiration suddenly strike or the mood to work overtake you, you are never out of the office. The downside is that however much you may feel the need to get away from work you are never out of the office. Equally, you are never out of your home which can be a mixed blessing. Taking this radical step should not be undertaken lightly, not least because if you share your home with anyone else you will automatically find yourself sharing your office. It can be lovely to feel at home while you are at work and particularly great if you are the sort who works best while glued to the television, but it does heighten the call on your powers of self-discipline. It is also time for a reality check because very, very few people really work best when they are glued to the television – although it is all too easy to convince yourself otherwise.

So if you have a will of iron and powers of concentration that could shatter glass, a merging of your work and life spaces may just work for you. But for the vast majority of home-alone soloists, a clear life space/work space separation works much better than an attempted synergy.

Case study

'When I started working from home I decided to enjoy my new freedom to the full and stacked all my work on a small table next to my favourite armchair. Why work sitting at a desk when you can be more comfortable? Then I started watching television while I worked. It was great – until I realized that my productivity had halved (or worse) compared to working in an office. Now I sit at my desk to work every day and my productivity is back up to 100 per cent.'

KEY THINGS TO REMEMBER

▶ *Establish a clear physical demarcation between your 'home' and your 'work', which is acceptable to everyone with whom you live.*

▶ *Ring-fence your time to ensure you avoid unnecessary interruptions while you are at work.*

▶ *With the other members of your household, agree some simple rules about when it is and is not acceptable for them to interrupt you – and make sure you abide by this too and do not succumb to the temptation of interrupting them!*

▶ *Try adopting a 'closed office door' policy.*

▶ *Do not skimp on creating an optimal work space. Spend the time and money necessary to provide an environment which will allow you to focus 100 per cent on your new career. Any costs incurred are very likely to be recouped very quickly.*

▶ *Clean and tidy your office, or arrange to have it cleaned and tidied, on a regular basis.*

▶ *Find the means to keep your home space and work space separate in your mind even if you have no choice but to have them physically merge.*

▶ *Ensure that when you are at work you do not allow your home life to impinge on your work life.*

8

Accentuating the positives of being your own boss

In this chapter you will learn:
- *what the advantages of 'small' are*
- *about the pros and cons of making the rules*
- *how to use downtime to your advantage*

The advantages of small

> **'Entrepreneurs and their small enterprises are responsible for almost all the economic growth in the United States.'**
>
> Ronald Reagan

As we have already seen there can be both significant upsides and significant downsides to being your own boss and working on your own or as part of a very small team, so you will need to learn how to maximize the advantages while minimizing the disadvantages. The trick is to turn every difference between your working life and situation and that of a big corporation to your advantage:

▶ *You are smaller so you cannot outgun them – but being smaller makes you more flexible.*

▶ *You are less established and less well-known – which means you are fresher and can offer something genuinely new and different.*

- *You are on your own – so you are not slowed down by an inefficient chain of command. You can make decisions quickly and begin acting on them immediately.*
- *You probably do not have swanky offices – which makes you more cost-effective (this also saves the time and expense of commuting which you can pass on to your clients to make you more competitive still).*

Of course these are only a few examples and the exact advantages and disadvantages will vary from business to business and from person to person, but the rule of thumb remains constant. By focusing on your strengths as a small enterprise and any large competitors' weakness as a big enterprise (which are often the same thing) you can often turn the situation to your advantage, and while you would be foolish to go toe to toe with them in a straight fight you might be able to capitalize on your speed and mobility to win projects ahead of them, or to take on the projects which they deem too small and fiddly.

The advantages of making the rules

There are also advantages and disadvantages to being your own boss versus being in someone else's paid employ and we have already looked at many of the pros and cons. Unfortunately, however, it is far easier to recognize the negative aspects than it is to see the positive aspects, so let us take a closer look at some of the advantages to being your own boss and making your own rules.

- *You can work your own hours/days/weeks, however it best suits you, so take full advantage of it. Provided you are getting as much work done as you need to for your business to be successful, then why not enjoy your new-found flexibility and adopt the work patterns of which you have always dreamed?*
- *You can dress, and indeed behave the way you want to. Fed up with having to wear a smart business outfit to work? Prefer to work in jeans, your pyjamas or even completely nude?*

(According to some surveys this applies to as many as 20 per cent of people who work from home!) Then what is stopping you? Now you can do exactly as you please and who knows, it may even help to boost your output and your profitability.

▶ *The increased flexibility you gain once you become your own boss means you can take as many breaks as you want, whenever you want, and go wherever you want to enjoy them. You might even decide to head into town and sit in a coffee shop while you complete your afternoon's work. Just be careful that you are completing as much work as you need to and that the quality is not suffering.*

▶ *Being your own boss allows you to achieve a better work/ life balance so take full advantage of it. If you have always dreamed of having more time to spend with your family and spending less time sat at your desk then take this opportunity to seize your chance.*

▶ *Do not forget to stop every so often and enjoy a moment of quiet reflection, remembering how much you hated always having someone looking over your shoulder and breathing down your neck, and that now you are your own boss you are answerable and accountable only to yourself.*

▶ *Take the time to review your finances to remind yourself that now you are keeping all the rewards of your hard efforts – even if you are not earning as much as you did when salaried. It will still feel sweeter.*

▶ *You always wanted to experience the feeling that everything is possible and that it is up to you to make it happen – so seize the day!*

▶ *You are no longer constrained to focusing on the narrow remit of your previous job, so make the most of the opportunity to pursue more creative and imaginative work interests.*

▶ *You can schedule your working life to benefit from an increase in quality time when and where it counts. Perhaps you have always wanted to take up a new hobby or pastime? Well now you can.*

▶ *Enjoy the challenge of being your own boss. There is no doubting that the challenge is a massive one but with it comes the opportunity for massive self-growth on all levels – personal, spiritual and emotional. So make the most of your new found*

*self-empowerment and take the time to reflect on your situation
every now and then and remind yourself why you wanted to
become your own boss in the first place and make sure that it is
helping to shape your life positively.*

▶ *You can pick and choose the work you want to do.*

Case study

'I think that my most uncomfortable moment was a piece
of work for a huge company that was a former nationalized
industry/utility. They were a nightmare – incredibly
bureaucratic, inconsiderate and demanding. But the great
thing is – I know that now and don't have to work for them
again if I choose not to.'

The disadvantages of making the rules

Although it is often easier to see the disadvantages than the
advantages, taking a close look at them not only helps the
newcomer to being their own boss forearm themselves, but in
some cases it can even highlight how you can turn the tables,
and turn a disadvantage into an advantage.

▶ **The fear of loneliness** *is often cited as one of the greatest
anxieties experienced by people who are considering
becoming their own boss. Given that most people will be
making the transition to working for themselves, and quite
possibly on their own, from the background of working in
a large office surrounded by colleagues this is completely
understandable. However, working alone does not mean
you have to be lonely; in today's 24/7 culture you can be in
touch with ex-colleagues, friends and so on as often as you
want to be.*

- ▶ **Being faced with a blank canvas** *where it is up to you (and destiny) to paint the picture – and your future. This can seem daunting but its effect is markedly lessened if you have a clear vision and a defined roadmap for your business.*
- ▶ **The fear of isolation** *is very real for many people when they first become their own boss, but working for yourself and even on your own need not be isolating. There are, for instance, a great many workshops and courses you can attend which will help to broaden your skill set as well as helping you to network, and even going out for a walk in the park or going to the gym will bring you into contact with other people.*
- ▶ **Loss of IT infrastructure/support.** *Becoming your own boss means you will have to set up an IT infrastructure, probably from scratch, but this gives you the opportunity to install a set-up which precisely matches your requirements.*
- ▶ **Financial insecurity** *is a worry to the vast majority of people when they first become their own boss, and for some people it is a potential problem which is never fully resolved – often despite the fact that cash flow and overall liquidity are not a problem. The trick, though it is devilishly difficult to master, is to look past your finances and at your business structure; if this is sound then why shouldn't your business remain profitable over the long term, even if you experience the occasional dip?*
- ▶ **Loss of structure.** *Becoming your own boss automatically means a loss of the structure with which you will have become familiar and perhaps on which you will have become dependent, but this gives you the opportunity to create a new structure for yourself, one which really works for you.*
- ▶ **Loss of external input/influence.** *This can be a mixed blessing, but try to focus on the lack of annoying input and disruptive influence and remind yourself every time you feel yourself yearning for some guidance that when it was available it was often the last thing you wanted! Also, by building up a network of other solo workers in a profession similar to your own you can always call on them for their input when you feel the need, just as you will always be there for them when they call.*

▶ **Risk.** *This is an unavoidable factor for everyone who decides to become their own boss but you can take steps to manage it, financially and emotionally.*

Case study

'I call it the "cup of tea syndrome". There is no one to make you a cup of tea and that applies to everything. So you have to get focused on a) what you are good at and b) what you aren't and ensure you get help with the latter ...'

Downtime and how to use it to your advantage

In learning to enjoy to the full the advantages of being your own boss and successfully managing your new lifestyle there is one area in which the vast majority of people fall down, an area of crucial importance, and as such it is worthy of special note.

GROW AN 'OFF' SWITCH

When you become your own boss you are, to all intents and purposes, your business – and there is a definite temptation to be at work, or at least on standby, every minute of every day of every year. Whether it is trying to crack a problem on the latest project or trying to think of creative new routes to getting the projects in the first place, whether it is trying to decide how best to handle a client or wondering whether it is time to chase that outstanding invoice yet again, the temptation to be 'at work' can be very strong indeed. Which is when you need to have an 'off' switch. It can be remarkably difficult to do, especially when you first become your own boss as it can seem as if you are not working as hard as you should be and if your business fails as a result you will have only yourself to blame. The truth, however, is that you will work more efficiently and more effectively if you build some rest periods into your work cycle. Quite simply, you need some downtime. *Everyone* needs some downtime. Do not fall into the trap of feeling you need to be working 24/7/365 if your business is to thrive, nor that you are the one person who can get away without having some time away from your business.

YOU NEED TO GET OUT MORE

This mistaken belief that as your own boss you need to work around the clock all year long is perhaps seen most starkly when it comes to taking – or not taking – holidays. Indeed what should be a real benefit and a joy instead becomes an absolute millstone. While it is quite natural, especially at first, to feel apprehensive about leaving your business for any length of time, if you want your business to thrive in the long term you must learn to take holidays; and that means actually *taking* holidays. Do not fall into the trap of thinking that it would be a good idea to take a holiday, perhaps even planning a holiday, before deciding that you cannot, that your business might grind to a halt or fall apart if you are not there to babysit it every second of every day. Depending on your line of work you may or may not be able to leave the business for three or four weeks at a stretch, but you can certainly afford a long weekend here and there; what is more, by going during the downtimes, which often cannot be predicted, you can ensure you get some fantastic last-minute deals so it need not cost the earth. And you get the smug satisfaction of knowing that you could never have just gone on a whim like that when you were in someone else's paid employ!

> 'After all, the best part of a holiday is perhaps not so much to be resting yourself, as to see all the other fellows busy working.'
>
> Kenneth Grahame

Alternatively, if you have the luxury of planning your holidays well in advance then you can take advantage of going out of season, another great way to keep costs down. Either way, it is certain that most of us fall into the trap of vastly overestimating the need our business has for our constant presence. What we should concentrate on is learning to trust the structure we have built up. We need to learn to let go, knowing that it will only be for a short while and understanding that the business will still be there when we return, and with advances in communications technology letting go need not mean losing touch. Mobile phones (cell phones) have enabled us to stay perpetually in contact, laptops mean we can carry our entire office in our suitcase, and Blackberries and iPhones etc. can bring our email to the beach. The trick is not to go on holiday only to continue exactly as if you were at home with only the different scenery reminding you that you are supposed to be on holiday, but actually to take a break and use the communications crutches only to respond to urgent client calls and any *real* emergencies which may occur. Many people, particularly in the early days (and even years) of being their own boss are like a nervous new parent with their business, scared of leaving their baby for even a few seconds. So learn to let go. A holiday from your business can be a good thing not only for your wellbeing but also for that of your company. By distancing yourself from the day-to-day routine you can often gain some very valuable insight into how to move your company forward or even to realize that it is not moving in the desired direction or at the required speed and some quality time away can give you the perspective you need to determine an action plan to get it back on track.

KEY THINGS TO REMEMBER

▶ *Being your own boss means your business will be tiny compared to the big corporations with which you might be in competition – and this can work to your advantage.*

▶ *It is important to understand those areas in which being small is an advantage and those areas in which being small is a disadvantage – and how to maximize the former while minimizing the latter.*

▶ *Once you are your own boss you make all the rules, which can be a double-edged sword.*

▶ *Making a virtue out of the necessity of making your own rules is vital to the success of your new business.*

▶ *You will almost certainly put in more hours as your own boss than you ever did while working for someone else, but it is important that you find the time to distance yourself from your business in order to gain real perspective. Use this insight to enable you to see where your business is going and to make any necessary alterations in your plans for its future.*

▶ *You may well experience periods of downtime in your new business, sometimes protracted, but you can turn these to your advantage.*

▶ *Do not fall into the trap of thinking that you cannot leave your business even for a short while to enable you to have a break or go on holiday. You can and you should.*

9

Maximizing home–office potential

In this chapter you will learn:
- *how to keep active while working from home*
- *how to avoid distractions and deal with loneliness*
- *about workplace discipline and security*

Exercise at work

'If it weren't for the fact that the TV set and the refrigerator are so far apart, some of us wouldn't get any exercise at all.'
Joey Adams

Once you begin to work from home your commute to work disappears, or at the most it involves moving to a different part of the house or to the summer house at the end of the garden. This is definitely a double-edged sword; it saves you a considerable amount of extra time but it significantly decreases the amount of activity you get each day, which is bad news for positive mental stimulus, for keeping your brain healthy and for keeping your outlook and your ideas fresh. It has long been upheld that a healthy body equals a healthy mind and if you want to keep your brain as active and agile as possible you could do a lot worse than keeping your body the same way. So perhaps a better expression of what we need to achieve is:

An active body = an active mind

So build into your day, or at the very least into your week, time and space to stretch those limbs, limber up those muscles, muscle your way into the local swimming baths and swim, or go out for a cycle, ice skate, roller blade, run, pump iron, swing an iron, do the ironing (vigorously) or whatever exercise you find most enjoyable and most beneficial. But whatever your fitness poison is, give yourself a large dose because it really does make a huge difference to your ability to function at your best. Taking an hour off for exercise every day will:

- *blow away the cobwebs of your current project*
- *help to give you perspective on current work and your business as a whole*
- *release endorphins to make you feel good*
- *get you out of the house, away from your desk and provide you with a change of scene*
- *get your blood pumping*
- *give you a mental break*
- *give your batteries an instant recharge*
- *allow you to spend time getting fitter instead of fatter*
- *keep you healthy*
- *release tension, particularly if your gym is equipped with a punch bag (which you might like to name!).*

Above all, it keeps those grey cells active, helping to keep you and your business on the front foot.

Insight

Being sat at your desk all day every day is a recipe for stagnation, both of your mind and of your business. So get up, get out, and get exercising to breathe some new life into both.

One of the major obstacles, of course, is finding the time to exercise but if you think you cannot afford to devote some of your working day to keeping your body and your mind fit then ask yourself this simple question – can you afford not to? If you spend the majority of your working life sitting at a desk, sedentary, then while you want and need to be as productive as possible for your business, you are actively (or should that be inactively?!) constraining yourself in such a way as to make this virtually impossible. The good news is that to rectify the situation does not require that you change into your gym gear, get into your car and head off for an hour's workout, followed by a shower, then another drive home, all of which will probably take two hours which you quite probably really do not have time for every day. Instead, all that is needed is a quarter of an hour to devote to a workout – and you do not even need to leave your desk to do it. So even if you find it impossible to find the time to get out of the house to get some exercise you really have no excuse not to build an exercise break into your daily routine, and just 15 minutes can make all the difference to how you feel, to your energy levels and your ability to give your best to your business.

There are a plethora of published exercise routines which can help, one of the most famous being that by the Royal Canadian Air Force: *Exercise Plans For Physical Fitness*, which describes an exercise system for 'shut-ins' (originally developed for pilots) comprising five basic exercises that are designed to work all the major muscle groups as well as the heart. Bear in mind that it is not designed to help you to lose a lot of weight or to train for a marathon, but simply to retain a minimal level of cardiovascular and muscular fitness. The exercises can be completed at your desk since they only require a space approximately 1 × 2 metres, and they are easy to remember and graded so that you can progress steadily. You can even do them when you are away on business trips since they only takes 15 minutes, require no equipment and are designed so that you will not break into a sweat when you do them so you can crowbar them into even the busiest of days when the only available time you have is just before a meeting. For more information, try www.gettingfitagain.com or www.goodbyecouch.com.

Insight

Exercising at your desk may sound a little strange and conjure odd images of office aerobics, but actually it makes perfect sense – keeping your mind healthy is vital to business success, whatever your business, and as you do not even need to leave your office and it only takes 15 minutes each day, you really do have the time to fit it into your work life. What you do not have is an excuse not to.

If for whatever reason you feel you simply cannot find a quarter of an hour each day to devote to exercise then you should still attempt to complete a 15-minute exercise routine – just break it up into five or six two-to-three-minute mini sessions and spread it throughout the day. By finding just a few minutes at a time to exercise you can still benefit from all the advantages of keeping active. Just get up and do it whenever the mood takes you using these quick energizers to relieve some stress, get your body active and your mind turbocharged. In this way you can choose whichever exercise suits your mood at that precise moment, using them to provide convenient, frequent breaks throughout the day, freeing your mind and spurring you to greater creativity.

Insight

If you are of the 'PlayStation generation' (and even if you are not), a Wii console can be a great way to keep your mind and body active. There are several fitness games available and these will not only help to keep you fit and active but they also provide a mental stimulus as well as acting as a great motivational tool.

Another great way to keep fit and healthy is to invest in a pedometer. Now that you do not have a commute, an office on the eighth floor or even a decent walk to the water cooler, you will need to find other ways to burn off those excess calories. If you ever wore a pedometer when you were in paid employment you were probably amazed at just how many steps you took every day. Wear one now that you work from home and you will be amazed at how few you take. The recommended minimum is 10,000 steps per day and in the course of an average day as an employee it is perfectly possible to cover this many as a matter of course, without even realizing it. As a home-alone worker however you probably won't even clock up 1,500 steps unless you make a concerted effort to do so. Investing in a pedometer provides a great fillip – it is wonderfully motivating so see how many steps you have managed, what this equates to in miles/kilometres covered, and how many calories you have burned as a result. It also acts as a constant reminder to put in the effort to cover some more ground – even if it is just walking in circles around your office. Better still, if you can find the time to go out for a walk you can get some fresh air while you burn calories and with a greatly reduced likelihood of getting dizzy!

Insight

Remember that being at home all day every day means you are never far from a mouth-watering selection of tempting foods and it is far too easy to rationalize their always being at hand as being one of the perks of being your own boss, and their consumption as necessary to provide the energy you need to feed your brain. If you want to remain in good shape once you work from home you will need to create some rigid rules for yourself about snacking!

Commuting (to the room next door)

One of the great benefits about being your own boss if you opt to work from home is that you no longer have to face the dreaded twice-daily commute, but ironically building a commute back into your working day might well be one of the most beneficial things you can do, providing an invaluable spur to your working life. The key reason for this is that it provides a physical and mental division between your home life and your work life, giving you an endpoint to being 'at home' and a starting point to being 'at work,' crucial now that physically these occupy the same space. It is a good idea to get into a routine for all aspects of your working life and nowhere is this more important than by beginning every day with a brisk walk. How far and how fast you go is completely up to you, but it need not be more than a ten-minute walk around the block to be beneficial, it just needs to be enough to begin your working day, to wake you up and blow away the cobwebs with a blast of fresh air, creating a clear demarcation point that allows you mentally to separate your home space from your work space and your home life from your work life. This will allow you to leave behind whatever baggage you may have there (be it good or bad) so that you arrive at the office turbo-charged and ready to go.

A physical journey is also a great aid to the mental transition required to put you firmly into the mindset of being a worker heading to work. By seeing everyone else on their journey to work you are reminded that this applies to you too. Yes, you are your own boss now, you make the rules and you even enjoy the luxury of working from home, but if your business is to thrive you need to remind yourself that first and foremost you are a worker, you have a job to do and a place of work from which to do it. So use the time on your 'commute' to really make the transition. Try to think of all the things in your home life which could have a negative effect on your working day – and then put them to one side. Very deliberately putting them in the 'Home Life' file in your head and putting them somewhere where they will not disturb you for the next eight or so hours is a great way to clear your head of unwanted distractions, allowing you to focus single-mindedly on your business.

Next, order your thoughts for the working day ahead: what needs to be accomplished? By when? What do you need to do in order to make it happen? In what order should you tackle the various tasks? What is the single most important thing you need to accomplish today? What is the *very first thing* you should be getting on with the minute you get to the office? Then keep this task at the front of your mind when you get back and make sure you go directly to your office and do it. Also, be sure to make it something positive and proactive. Do not deliberately provide yourself an easy run-in with something like, 'Check my emails' or, 'Look up that certain something on the web I thought of yesterday that might, just possibly, one day, prove to be vaguely useful should a certain set of unlikely circumstances ever occur'. Instead make it a definite task with a measurable outcome and a clear endpoint to slingshot you into your day.

Insight

Do not allow yourself to be sidetracked. The minute you have stepped in through the door you have arrived at work so head straight for your office – if you go via the kitchen to make a cup of coffee or stop to sort through the post or go anywhere else to do anything else other than dive headlong into your working day you will risk losing the valuable momentum the commute has given you.

Avoiding prevarication and transference

It is time to put the monkey back on your shoulder. Most of us write 'To Do' lists of the required tasks for the day/week/year ahead. It is a great way of getting organized and prioritizing our workload, and there is a wonderful sense of satisfaction in completing the tasks and then crossing them off the list. However – and it is a big 'however' – this only works if the lists and the timeframes are kept short. Making long lists of things you plan to achieve is a fantastic way of ensuring you never do.

Quite simply, long lists = transference; and transference = getting nowhere fast.

THE 'TRANSFERENCE TRAP'

This is the 'transference trap'. Compiling lists may make you feel better, but what does it actually achieve? Without proper management, very little; worse – it fools you into feeling that you are making great strides when in reality you are barely toddling.

'Reorganizing can be a wonderful method for creating the illusion of progress while producing confusion, inefficiency, and demoralization.'

Petronius Arbiter

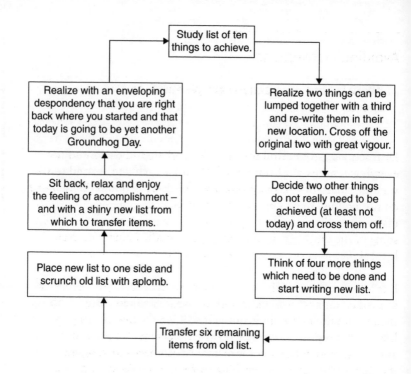

AVOIDING THE TRAP

Follow these simple rules in order to avoid the transference trap:

▶ *Keep your lists short and relevant.*
▶ *Ensure they only include tasks which really are achievable.*
▶ *Prioritize them and work from the top down focusing on just one task at a time.*
▶ *Make sure that you see each task through to completion before moving on to the next.*

Remember that simply writing the lists themselves accomplishes nothing and compiling an endless series of lists is a recipe for failure since the very act of writing them gives you a false sense of reassurance that the tasks are on their way to being accomplished.

Avoiding distractions

'Work is hard. Distractions are plentiful. And time is short.'

Adam Hochschild

Distractions are plentiful for the solo worker, and doubly so for everyone who works from home. We are magnets to myriad time-wasting sidetracks and unproductive cul-de-sacs, and if distractions do not find us we will find them – or even create them; and just to make life really difficult, they are not always easy to spot. Indeed, some of the most pernicious can appear totally benign, or even helpful. Let us take an example – housework.

It is all too easy to notice a cobweb in the corner of your office or some dust on a filing cabinet and to dispatch yourself there and then to put the matter in hand. After all, surely that is just good house-keeping? En route to getting the vacuum cleaner or duster and polish you notice some crockery which needs loading into the dishwasher, a pile of washing waiting to be done (and then ironed), and that you are nearly out of milk. Not to mention the dripping tap that needs seeing to, and the windows which need cleaning, and … Before you know it the working day will have become the evening and you will be no further forward with your business than you were before breakfast. It is incredibly easy to be distracted in this way and just about everyone who becomes their own boss is guilty of it from time to time, but it is a real trap and a real time waster. So how do you combat it? First and foremost you need to stay focused on the fact that while you might be in your house you are not at home – you are at work, in the office. Try to imagine that you are still in someone else's paid employ, working in a busy office and apply the rules and working practices which would be right for that environment to your new working life. How many times during your erstwhile paid employ did you put aside the project on which you were working to suddenly grab the vacuum cleaner from the cleaners' cupboard or equip yourself with a mop and bucket and set about cleaning your office? Exactly.

And if it would not have been acceptable there, in the office while you were at work, then it should not be acceptable when you work from home, in the office while you are at work.

Quite simply, while you are at work, work. Vacuuming, dusting, doing the washing, feeding the cat, loading the dishwasher, unloading the dishwasher, shopping for the evening meal before the rest of the family gets home, preparing the evening meal before the rest of the family gets home, eating the evening meal before the rest of the family gets home – whatever it is you are tempted to do, if it would not fit the day-to-day working life of a large multinational then leave it. They are all chores which are necessary evils but they are chores which are part of your home life not your work life, which means they can wait – can and must – until you get home from work, not physically but mentally.

The loneliness of the long-distance worker

For a lot of people one of the major drawbacks to becoming their own boss is the lack of a social element to their work life and never is this more keenly felt than during the downtimes in your working day. While you are hard at work you will probably be too busy working to notice or care, but as soon as you take a break, particularly your lunch break, you may well find the silence to be deafening and where in your previous paid employment you may well have gone out for lunch with some colleagues you now find yourself stuck at home, alone. Take a moment to think back to when you worked for someone else and with someone else (or quite possibly a lot of people): did you sit at your desk every day to eat your lunch? Or did you go out somewhere, at least every once in a while, perhaps to a local restaurant or café, or to get some take-out sandwiches from a good deli to eat in the park and enjoy a change of scene. Maybe you would go with a colleague or two and try to talk about anything but work, or if you did find the conversation wandering back to the company you can be sure it was to gossip, not to discuss work plans. And on those occasions when you did stay in the office building you were probably keen to at least make sure that you got away from your desk for some of your break – to the canteen, common room, lounge etc.

So what is the difference now?

You work for yourself and quite possibly by yourself, but that does not have to mean that you never meet anyone for lunch. You may work from home but that does not mean that you cannot ever leave it. You craved a social element to your working life then and you need it just as much now – so make sure you get it. One of the disadvantages to being your own boss is that it will take more time and effort to engineer so it is probably not practical to try to do it every day but you should certainly be able to find time to go out and meet someone for lunch at least once a week. Use it as a natural opportunity to network, affording you the opportunity to grow your business whilst enjoying someone else's company, and you will even be able to claim it as a business expense! (Better still, get them to pay!) On those occasions when you will have to enjoy your own company there is still no reason not to get out and enjoy a change of scene. A good idea is to train yourself to engage in distractions (watch television, read a book, listen to some music) and mentally move out of the workplace. Of course you will need to be disciplined to avoid taking breaks when you should not and this can be a difficult habit to get used to – but so can forcing yourself to take breaks when you should.

Learn from your previous work life. Although there are many advantages to being your own boss which you should enjoy to the full, not least a new-found flexibility in your work life, it is all too easy to take advantage of your situation to the detriment of your business.

Insight

A good rule of thumb for what is and what is not appropriate in your new career is to think about a large multinational and see whether whatever behaviour or action you are considering would be considered acceptable or advantageous there. If it

(Contd)

would then it is probably going to be good for your business too; if it would not then you need to think long and hard about your reasons for wanting to do it before committing yourself.

Workplace discipline and security

As soon as you become your own boss you need to implement a strict regime of workplace discipline and good practice in order to ensure your company functions to its maximum capacity all the time, with rigorous safeguards in place to prevent data loss or theft, or malicious damage, and to streamline your working practices for maximum efficiency. Many of the safeguards you need to employ and the good habits which you need to make routine in your day-to-day working life will have been unnecessary in your former work life if you were employed by a large company since they will have had robust measures in place to protect you and your work which did not involve your direct input. Indeed, you may not even have been aware of their presence. Now that the buck for everything stops with you, however, you need to assume responsibility for your company's security as well as that of your clients on those occasions when you are made privy to sensitive data.

Do you need to buy a shredder? If you do not already have one located in your work space then the answer is 'Yes'. You may well already have one for domestic purposes, but in terms of security you need to ensure that the shredder you use for your business is located in your office and used only by you. You also need to make sure that it is man enough for the job (it must be a crosscut shredder so that materials are not simply cut vertically into long thin strips but are also cut horizontally so that any sensitive hard copy data is quickly transformed into tiny, meaningless short shreds) and that it can cope with more than just paper, for those occasions when you need to dispose of card, celluloid etc. This also has the additional benefit of allowing you to shred thin sheet data in large quantities. If you expect to have a lot of data of which you need to dispose then it is also advisable to invest in a shredder whose receptacle capacity negates the need to empty it every five minutes as this will only deter you from shredding everything which you know ought to be shredded. Finally, a shredder in your office is a permanent presence and a constant reminder to keep on top of your paperwork and prevent it turning into a paper mountain, to clear the decks on a regular basis and to implement tight workplace security.

> **'Throw the lumber over, man! Let your boat of life be light ...'**
> Jerome K. Jerome, *Three Men in a Boat*

In the same way that you need to keep your desk cleared of the sea of paperwork which will otherwise threaten to drown you, so you need to treat your hard drive in much the same way. By deleting sensitive data that is no longer required you will keep on top of security while at the same time freeing up your hard drive.

Insight

Do not forget that deleting information from your computer and even formatting the hard drive does not get rid of the data; instead, it simply tells your computer that this information is no longer required and the areas in which it is stored can now be used. Thus the data which you have deleted will remain on your hard drive until it is overwritten. If you want to remove it permanently from your computer you will need to use a programme such as 'Eraser' to wipe it clean to 'factory new' status.

On the other side of the coin, but no less important to the solo worker, is the need to ensure that all work is properly protected from corruption or unwanted deletion and that it is securely backed up. This really is an area in which lazy people take the most pains as anyone will know who has ever had a computer crash terminally with an irrevocable loss of data, or suffered the loss of a PDA/mobile phone. Often people do not realize just how important the information is and how lost they would be without it until it is too late. Worse still, an irretrievable loss of data could mean an inability to complete a piece of work for a client, resulting in a loss of revenue and sharply diminishing your prospects of ever being asked to work for them again. Happily the answer is simple and straightforward and the process is easy to accomplish. The only tricky bit is remembering to do it!

To back-up a computer you will need to invest in an external hard drive to which you can write all necessary data and you should get into the habit of doing this on a regular basis. Exactly how often will depend on the speed and regularity at which you gather and store new information; for some people it is a task which needs to be undertaken every few hours, for others it is sufficient to do it once a week. The same principle goes for any other devices on which you store information.

Insight

Whatever your line of work, try to ensure that you back up your hard drive and any other data storage devices at least once a week. This really should be the maximum length of time you leave it because getting into the habit of backing up your data regularly is the only way to ensure it never gets forgotten, overlooked or postponed until it is too late causing a potentially disastrous loss.

Surely the easiest way to ensure your data is protected is to utilize the automatic back-up software with which most external hard drives come. This enables them to back up automatically a specified hard drive or hard drives once you have determined the regularity with which you wish this task to be performed. Utilizing this option is an excellent way to ensure that the task always gets done, and on time, but the operation can be intrusive (and sometimes noisy) so make sure that you bear this in mind when determining the days and times at which you want this to occur.

Insight

If you need to back up data on an ad hoc basis it can be useful to use an extra, smaller storage device such as a USB flash drive (sometimes called a USB memory stick). This operation is usually much quicker than using a full external hard drive and brings with it the benefit of portability. It can also act as a second backup storage device for any vitally important data.

This belt and braces approach can work well if you get into the habit of backing up the projects on which you are currently working to both storage devices. Just remember to keep them in separate locations.

As well as backing up all your important data it is a good idea to get into the habit of giving your computer a weekly 'spring clean'. Whether you do this at the same time as backing up your data, or whether you prefer to keep these tasks separate (particularly if you have set up the 'fire and forget' automatic back-up to run during the night), giving your computer a regular service will help to keep it running at its most efficient allowing your business to do the same. Obviously the number and nature of the tasks required will vary from business to business, but there are three key tasks which you should always try to accomplish as a minimum:

1   **Update any virus protection software you have installed.** *The requirements for this are largely dependent on the operating system you use and to some extent the number and nature of internet searches your business requires you to make, but whatever your situation it is worth erring on the side of caution. It is certainly better to have too much protection than too little since the consequences of a malware invasion on your system can be devastating and keeping on top of the latest software threats on a regular basis is your best defence. The threat from hackers and those who get their kicks writing malicious software never takes a week off, so neither should you.*

2   **Defragment your hard drives and empty any unwanted cache, folders etc.** *Keeping your system clean in this way not only helps to make it easier to navigate your hard drives and to see where things are at a glance, it will also improve your system's speed and efficiency. Not developing good habits in this respect will impair your system over time making you less*

efficient and your work more laborious. *Another benefit to regular defragmentation of your hard drives is an increase in their storage capacity.*

3 **Ensure you know where everything on your computer is and revisit any folders the contents of which you are unsure or which you had forgotten about completely!** *This really is well worth doing once you are your own boss since even the most efficient of people will find that getting into this routine sometimes produces unexpected results.*

Case study

'It wasn't until I went through my hard drives for the first time, carefully checking all my folders and subfolders, that I realized just how much was there that I'd forgotten about, or didn't remember ever knowing. It took me a couple of days and was boring, tedious work but the results proved well worth it because I came across folders I'd long since forgotten about – and in some cases, clients! I immediately set about making amends, more clearly labelling folders and putting them where they should be, and contacting the clients I had rediscovered. Now I go through this process every Friday morning to ensure I don't make the same mistakes again and it only takes me about 20 minutes ...'

KEY THINGS TO REMEMBER

▶ *Once you become your own boss it is very easy to take less and less exercise – even though mental stimulation through physical exertion is more important than ever.*

▶ *Engineering a 'commute' to work not only gives you some fresh air and exercise at the beginning of your working day but also provides a valuable opportunity to leave behind your home life and arrive at the office in 'work mode'.*

▶ *Prevarication and transference are two of the biggest dangers to everyone who works for themselves. Learning to spot these two imposters, and to successfully manage them, is vital to the success of your business.*

▶ *Distractions are plentiful for the solo worker, particularly if you work from home. You will need to develop an iron will and implement a disciplined workplace routine in order to keep your business on track.*

▶ *Loneliness and isolation are two of the most commonly experienced negative aspects to solo working and all too often go unnoticed until they become a real problem. Keep an eye out for warning signs and remember that prevention is better than cure.*

▶ *It is easy to allow the flexibility in your working life which you enjoy as your own boss to undermine the discipline crucial for the long-term success of your business. You will need to determine what is and what is not acceptable and establish and implement appropriate boundaries.*

▶ *The security of your business and sometimes that of your clients can be compromised if you do not employ rigorous workplace discipline.*

- *Lazy people take the most pains – ensure all your data is backed up on a regular basis.*

- *Get into the habit of 'spring cleaning' your hard drive regularly.*

10

....

Targets and planning

In this chapter you will learn:
- *how to create your business plan and roadmap*
- *how to set realistic targets*
- *problem-solving strategies*
- *how to project manage successfully*
- *ways to keep motivated*

Creating your business plan and roadmap

> **'In preparing for battle I have always found that plans are useless, but planning is indispensable.'**
>
> Dwight D. Eisenhower

A great many people who become their own boss mistakenly believe that because they are now flying solo they do not need to bother with planning for their business. The reality is that everyone who runs their own company, even – indeed especially – if that company comprises just them, needs to plan ahead, although it is true that conventional business plans are often of limited use. Instead, you need to discover the format for planning the success of your business which helps to create a self-fulfilling prophecy, albeit one which will not materialize without a lot of hard work from you. By creating a solid foundation on which to build your business you are laying yourself a platform for success. Since this cannot be done without thinking through all the major aspects of running your business, from establishing your business offer and consolidating your initial start-up plans, to how you will establish a broad client base and manage your cash flow, right through to understanding your ultimate goal and the timeframe for accomplishing it, structured planning from the outset will help you to keep your business on track and provide an excellent yardstick by which to measure its progress. Importantly you need to re-evaluate your business plan regularly to ensure it still provides a suitable framework to enable you to achieve the success you desire for your business.

A good business plan serves as a roadmap for your company and as such it needs to have a degree of flexibility built into it to accommodate unexpected twists and turns, but be careful not to allow this to become an excuse to keep your plans vague and woolly. Also remember that your business plan is organic and will evolve over time so do not be reluctant to take the leap to starting out as your own boss just because you do not feel that the plans you have created for your business are completely finalized. If you wait for them to be perfect you will be waiting a long time!

Planning your business year, quarter, month, week, and even day is critical to ensure your company is continually heading in the right direction, and at the required speed. It is far too easy (and commonplace) to get to a point on the calendar and wonder, in a regretful tone, where the year has gone – and why you did not reach any of the targets you set. It is vitally important to be crystal clear as to what you want to achieve, and by when, and although this might change as things evolve and circumstances dictate fluctuations in your anticipated course and speed, having a very clear vision and knowing the course you want to steer will enable you to keep track of your progress and keep things on target.

Setting realistic targets – optimism versus realism

> **'The pessimist complains about the wind; the optimist expects it to change; the realist adjusts the sails.'**
>
> William Arthur Ward

One of the key strategies to employ is to ensure the targets you set really are realistic given your available time, resources, prevailing market conditions, your experience and ability etc. Above all, be honest with yourself and be tough where you need to be. It will save a lot of unnecessary and completely avoidable disappointment later on. One school of thought suggests that the easiest way to ensure you always reach your targets, and to avoid disappointment, is simply to aim low! On the other hand, it is all well and good sitting down with a blank piece of paper (or the back of an envelope to 'update' your business plan every time you get bored) and outlining your five-year vision for the company, beginning with you, your laptop and bags of enthusiasm and ending with global business domination, but if your targets are not realistic then you are simply setting yourself up to fail. Worse still, you are creating a framework which could very well prevent you succeeding. There is nothing quite so de-motivating as periodically looking at where you are versus plan and knowing that you cannot possibly achieve your goals. Aiming unrealistically high is a great way to make you feel like a failure even if you are doing well. So be tough with yourself – are you really going to change the world? Well, you might, of course, in which case 'hello' to you Mr Gates, but for the rest of us being realistic means setting your sights a little lower and being content with improving things just a little – possibly the world, more likely just a bit of it, certainly your bank balance.

If, on the other hand, your targets are too low you will achieve them quickly and easily, leaving yourself nothing to shoot for and knowing in your heart that the only reason for your apparent success is that you cheated yourself in the first place – equally de-motivating. So you need to ensure your targets are as *realistic* as possible. What those are will, of course, depend on a huge number of factors unique to you and your business (starting capital, previous experience, pre-existing network of contacts etc.), and in the early years of being your own boss things can be very difficult to predict, but it is worth spending the necessary time to ensure you get them as accurate as possible and be prepared to revise them periodically.

Problem-solving strategies

Envisaging potential problems well ahead of time is much more important for a soloist or small start-up team than it is for large companies; they have the luxury of making mistakes – you do not. In planning your strategies and setting your targets try also to imagine worst-case scenarios for each stage. Go through a checklist of all the 'What if?' scenarios you can envisage and outline strategies for dealing with each one, including how to avoid them in the first place if possible.

What if...?	Coping strategy
One of your clients fails to pay on time.	Do you have funds sufficient to cope with the late payment? If not, you might need to arrange an overdraft facility to bridge the gap. If this is declined, what are your alternatives?
You are taken ill for a period of time, or suffer an accident.	Is there someone who can run the business for you, temporarily? Do you have adequate insurance in place for your business (e.g. liability insurance, overdraft interest protection) and personal (e.g. mortgage repayment protector, credit card payment insurance) to cover the financial

	losses? Are there clients who are relying on your output for their immediate business plans, and will a delay be acceptable to them? If not, how will you ensure you do not disappoint them in order to retain their goodwill and future business?
The cost of materials suddenly rises.	Will you be able to pass on the price increase to clients and still remain competitive? If not, how much of the increase can your business soak up without negatively impacting the profit margin to an unacceptable level? What if you have to operate at a loss for a while?

Of course the scenarios will vary from business to business and thus so must the coping strategies, so think through your business plans and try to determine all the likely pitfalls and pratfalls which might beset it and how you would deal with them if they occurred. Revisit this list every few weeks in the early stages of being your own boss and update it as necessary including any eventualities which have actually occurred. Over time you should find that you are needing to update your list less and less often and revisiting it every quarter will be sufficient.

Charting your position and plotting a profitable course

It might sound like odd advice, but as soon as you become your own boss one of the first things you should do is to go out and buy a wall planner. The reason is simple. Keeping your targets and your deadlines in sight (literally) at all times is a great way to ensure that not a day goes by when you are not reminded of where your company is, where it needs to be, and by when. If you start falling behind it is an inescapable reminder, which is no bad thing. It is also useful to have your entire year's targets and plans laid out before you so you can see the big picture at a glance, and it helps to prevent any looming targets or deadlines coming as a surprise. A word of caution though – once you have bought the wall planner make sure you actually get around to putting it up on the wall! It is incredible how many times you see virtually (or sometimes even completely) empty wall planners adorning the offices of the self-employed, often still rolled up and held tight with a smart rubber band. Let's face it, if you cannot even be bothered to keep your wall planner up to date (or even to put it up on the wall) you are unlikely to be bothered to chase work, impress clients, excel in projects and generally run a tight, focused business. You could even find a better use for the rubber band!

Insight

The road to business failure is paved with blank wall planners.

Ask yourself, why did you buy the wall planner in the first place? Chances are it was either because you were filled with the admirable intention of keeping it bang up to date throughout the year, thus aiding your ability to organize your business planning and to secure work and meet deadlines, or it was to cover up a large crack in the wall. Or maybe just because you were feeling guilty that you failed to fill in last year's. Whatever your reason, the point is that you *should* have a wall planner, and in a prominent position in your office because it really does help in keeping your business leading edge. It acts as a useful reminder of how much of the year has already gone (usually at an alarming rate) and how much – and thus how much opportunity – is left. Writing on it the key stages in the year and what you want to have achieved by each is a quick and easy way to show exactly where you are, and where you had intended (or hoped) to be. Thus it charts both your progress throughout the year, and your degree of under- or overachievement versus plan. Depending on how your year is going (and how realistic your targets were in the first place) it acts as carrot or stick, or both. It is a timekeeper, a motivator and an organizer. And it will cover up that crack.

WRITE YOUR OWN, AND YOUR COMPANY'S, OBITUARY

This is a self-actualizing exercise. Firstly, you need to write a brief paragraph describing how you and your company might be summed up on the day you retire, or sell it for a large profit:

▶ *What position will you hold?*
▶ *What will your day-to-day work comprise?*
▶ *What will your salary be?*
▶ *What will your company look like?*
▶ *What position will it occupy versus its rivals?*
▶ *How many people will it employ?*
▶ *What will your client roster comprise?*
▶ *What will your business be worth?*

Write it in as much detail as you feel is necessary to convey your business desires fully. It is your company, it is your vision, it is your dream. So go ahead and write the future. Prescribe all the elements of the rise and rise of your business. Ambition is no bad thing here, so by all means aim high – just remember you need to be realistic too. This document, if well thought out and pragmatic, should form a point of reference for you and your company for the future, a control chart against which you can map progress – but realism is crucial. If your targets were beyond the bounds of what might reasonably be achieved with a lot of hard work, dedication, and a pinch of good fortune, then its worth is dramatically diminished and you are simply setting yourself up for a fall.

As you can see from the following examples, obituaries can come in all shapes and sizes and they need not be long and complicated – just make sure that yours is the right length and complexity for your company.

Leading FTSE 100 company 'Over-achievers PLC' was founded in 2007 by the woman who was to remain at its helm for 14 years, before announcing her retirement yesterday. The charismatic Global CEO and President was responsible for charting its meteoric rise from a one-person company offering
(Contd)

bed and breakfast accommodation to an international chain of luxury hotels and resorts employing more than 12,000 staff. She retires as one of the world's richest women.

The pioneer behind the national accountancy consultants 'Abacus Ltd.' has announced he is taking early retirement at the age of 46. Having masterminded an entirely new form of accounting practice and auditing, he leaves behind one of the country's fastest growing companies and will remain a major shareholder.

The founder and head of a respected local window-cleaning company, Simon Simons (of Simons & Sons) has announced his retirement with immediate effect. Over the course of the last 37 years he has overseen the company's growth from just two people (Mr Simons and his son Simon) to one of the best respected companies in the area employing some 14 people.

Respected local calligrapher Rachel Russel has announced her retirement at the age of 54. Her beautiful inscriptions adorn many of the city's local buildings. She will be moving to France to enjoy her early retirement.

CHARTING YOUR POSITION

Next, you need to plot your current position. Below are some of the elements you might wish to consider:

- ▶ *Where is your company right now?*
- ▶ *What does it look like?*
- ▶ *How many people does it employ?*
- ▶ *What does your client roster comprise?*
- ▶ *What is your business worth?*

Again, you need to be completely honest and truthful and as accurate as you can be. This list need be for your eyes only so you are fooling no one but yourself if you pretend that your company is leagues ahead of where it really is. Equally, do not be tempted to understate your company's position just so that further down the track when you revisit this chart you can convince yourself that you are moving faster than you really are! A true and accurate picture of your real position at present may not make great reading straight after you have envisaged the future, but remember the whole point of this exercise is to determine the steps necessary in order to turn that vision into reality.

PLOTTING YOUR COURSE

Next you need to plot the points in between these two extremes:

▶ *How will you grow the company such as to be able to get from your current position to where you want to be?*
▶ *What are the necessary steps along the way?*
▶ *What stepping stones will you need to place to help you achieve this?*
▶ *Where will they be?*
▶ *Who will you need to get to help you and in what ways?*
▶ *What are the potential stumbling blocks and pitfalls along the way?*
▶ *What is the timescale over which this needs to be completed?*

Lastly, you simply need to join the dots. You know where you and your business are. You know where you want to be. You know the requisite steps along the way so know how you will achieve it. You know what assistance you will require and from whom, and you know the timescale for each. So you have everything you need to plot your company's course to its maximum growth potential and every reason to believe you can get it there.

Then broadcast your forecast.

Tell your friends, your family, your network of colleagues, even your clients, put it on your website – in fact tell anyone who will listen. Shout it from the rooftops, because letting everyone know your targets is a great way of providing the incentive to achieve them. No one likes to fall short of their targets – everyone loathes doing so publicly.

Project management

Whether you have just one project on the go and are actively
seeking to line up some more or already have several running
concurrently, it is vitally important that you run each one with
precision and care. Inept project management is a sure-fire way
to ensure that things are not accomplished in the best order
to maximize your time and that of anyone to whom you are
subcontracting, that clients feel uncertain about the likelihood of
a successful outcome, and even that deadlines are missed resulting
in unhappy clients or worse still, cancelled work and zero chance
of repeat business. Effective project management, on the other
hand, allows you to see exactly when and how each stage of the
process will be accomplished. The impression you want to convey
to the client is that their project is the only one you are handling
and that they have 100 per cent of your focus and expertise. By
planning, organizing and managing your resources effectively you
can combat the restraints of scope, time and budget to meet your
project goals and objectives.

Motivation

**'People who are unable to motivate themselves must be
content with mediocrity, no matter how impressive their
other talents.'**

Andrew Carnegie

The best way to motivate yourself once you are your own boss and there is no one to do it for you is to put a metaphorical gun to your head. Quite simply, it really is worth scaring yourself a little here. The thing is, unless you have never been employed except by yourself (in which case this may be because everyone else in the world thinks you are unemployable – just a thought) then it stands to reason that you have taken the very brave decision to abandon all the safety and security of a salaried job and risk everything to put yourself in the position you are now in. So it should be safe to assume you have some very compelling reasons for doing so. And what happens if your business fails? The bills will still have to be paid so in all probability you will have to abandon your new career and get a job, and you will have landed yourself right back where you started, in someone else's employ, working hard on their terms in order to line their pockets – only this time you will be cap in hand, dreams shattered and pride on the floor and knowing how much better life could – and should – have been with you as the boss. Every tiny niggle, every gripe, every reason you had for wanting out in the first place will be magnified exponentially. So seize this potent dream/nightmare combination and use it to your advantage. Envisaging a thriving business and planning ways to celebrate your success are one side of the motivational coin, but it can be just as motivating to remind yourself of all the unpleasant things with which you will be faced if your business fails. It can work wonders to have as a business spur a list to which you can refer every time you cannot be bothered to put in a full day's work, each time the going gets tough and you begin to wonder if it is all worth it. The contents of each soloist's list will of course vary, as will the length (though if you find yourself starting a third page you might want to consider seeking professional help) but to get you started here are a few of the more common reasons solo workers give for jettisoning the wage-slave life and becoming their own boss:

▶ *You hated the commute.*
▶ *You hated the office politics.*
▶ *You didn't like being told what to do.*
▶ *You wanted to create your own style for the business.*

- *You wanted to call the shots.*
- *You wanted flexibility in your working hours.*
- *You wanted a better work/life balance.*
- *You were fed up with putting in so much hard work to line someone else's pockets.*
- *You knew you could make a better job of it on your own.*
- *You just wanted to be your own boss.*

Of course there are pros as well as cons to conventional modes of working just as there are to being your own boss, but reminding yourself of the downsides every once in a while is a great way to provide extra motivation, particularly when the going gets tough in a way which would not have been problematic in your erstwhile employ. It is worth remembering, too, that the grass is always greener on the other side and of course you are going to wonder from time to time if it is worth all the aggravation: book-keeping; chasing work; working all hours and then having to chase the payments; weekends and bank holidays getting swallowed up as you work to make hay while the sun shines, and so on. But whenever negativity strikes take a moment to revisit your list and then close your eyes and put yourself back, just for a moment, into the wage-slave harness.

> **'People often say that motivation doesn't last. Well, neither does bathing – that's why we recommend it daily.'**
> Zig Ziglar

Remember the many aggravations, annoyances and petty niggles of your former working life – always having to do everything by the book (a book someone else had written), wishing you would get the credit you deserved, knowing that you were working hard only to line someone else's pocket, having to put up with the commute, the office politics, that certain 'someone' in the office, always dancing to someone else's tune, and so on. And when you have mentally put yourself firmly back in their world, in your old world, look across and see just how much greener the grass is on the other side. On your side. On the side of being your own boss. Then open your eyes and enjoy your freedom, even if it is not perfect all of the time. Even a bad day at the office when it is your company can be better than a good day at the office when it is someone else's.

SO MUCH FOR THE STICK – WHERE IS THE CARROT?

Working for yourself is hard – rewarding, but hard. And while the sense of achievement is consummately satisfying you need to give yourself a more tangible and immediate incentive for putting in the long hours, for the blood, the sweat and the tears. But you need to make it realistic. It is no good if you pretend that at the end of the project, when the client finally settles the invoice, you are going to buy yourself a new car if deep down you know it is never going to happen. Having long-term goals and even pipe dreams for when you make it really big, however, are an excellent idea – you just need to be clear that that is what they are. You also need to give yourself something realistic to shoot for in the short and medium term, however, something you really will do or buy at the end of each and every project (or batch of workpieces if they are all on the small side) – and if that happens to be a new car then so much the better. Or perhaps your end-of-year goal is to buy that car but the end-of-project prize is a more modest half day at the local go-kart track or a weekend away. Whatever they are, ensure your goals are attainable and then actually *do them* once the project is over. Looking back fondly on a great day out thanks to the dividends of the last project is an excellent way of providing motivation for current and future work.

Case study

'I have a hobby that I take seriously. I like powerboating. I make time in my diary to do it and enjoy every minute of it. This is not a weekend thing – it only takes time from my work diary. It is worth every minute as it energizes me for the client work when I do it. Without this I would get stale pretty quickly.'

We all know how incentivizing it is to have hard work recognized and rewarded, perhaps by your line manager, perhaps by your head of department, maybe by the boss him or herself – or even by all three. Well, now you are all those people, or to put it another way, if you don't do it no one else will. Think of it as the positive side of the buck always stopping here (you knew there had to be one eventually). So, incentivize yourself that if you achieve X by Y you will reward yourself with your chosen prize, a real, tangible reward not a half-hearted pat on the back and some hollow thanks. After all, you can't spend thanks. And since you know yourself rather well you can ensure you will get something you really want. And as for that pipe dream? Well, why not? After all, you might just sell your company to a large multinational one of these days, or float it on the stock market ...

MOTIVATIONAL CHART

	Current project	Quarter	Year end	Long term	Pipe dream
Completion date	30 April	30 June	31 December	within next ten years	before retirement
Client	Big Spenders Inc.	Big Spenders Inc. A & B Construction	Big Spenders Inc. A & B Construction X, Y, Z & Co At least two others	move from small-/ medium-size companies to blue chips	global blue chips and industry leaders
Project	Jazz	Jazz Starling Blue Train	min. six small-scale and two medium-scale	min. eight global projects per year	one mega project leading to sale of company for big bucks, then retirement
Reward	go-karting	day at the races	weekend at luxury hotel	Ferrari	Sunseeker luxury yacht

SPOIL YOURSELF – DO YOUR ACCOUNTS

Surprisingly, one of the biggest and most motivating boons for people who own and run their own company is doing the accounts. Keeping up to date with the company book-keeping is a necessary evil most of us put off and off until the last possible moment, by which time we have a paperwork mountain to climb, but if you find it impossible to break this cycle, even though each time you swear blind you will not let it happen again, try looking at it from a different perspective. Think of all the money you are making by doing your accounts. Or to put it another way, think of it as money you have already spent and now you are able to get some of it back as a gift from the government. Every legitimate business expense, provided it was incurred wholly and solely for the benefit of your business is tax deductible – so get busy with Excel and watch the savings grow. Not only does this mean you will motivate yourself with the thought of all the money you can reclaim but you will enjoy the added bonus of getting your accounts in early for once.

SELF-MOTIVATION

'You can motivate by fear. And you can motivate by reward. But both of these methods are only temporary. The only lasting thing is self-motivation.'

Homer Rice

Happily, as solo workers we can enjoy a great benefit in this respect. One of the great motivational boons to being your own boss is that since you are your company and must be self-reliant for everything it necessarily follows that all motivation is self-motivation. So use this advantage to the full and employ all the motivational techniques in this chapter, both stick and carrot, to keep yourself focused, energized and enthusiastic about your new career.

KEY THINGS TO REMEMBER

▶ *Establish your vision for your company and create a defined and realistic roadmap, with checkpoints at each major stage.*

▶ *Ensure your targets are neither falsely optimistic nor pessimistic, but realistic.*

▶ *Try to identify potential problems ahead of time and establish problem-solving strategies to deal with them.*

▶ *Keep your targets in plain view all the time, and review them as often as necessary.*

▶ *Plot your course to meeting your targets and review as necessary.*

▶ *Write long-term and short-term obituaries for yourself and your company.*

▶ *Tell friends, family, former colleagues etc. about your plans for your company to provide yourself with added motivation.*

▶ *List the reasons you quit your job to become your own boss and keep it somewhere prominent for frequent reference.*

▶ *Decide on some short- and long-term rewards for meeting targets and plan them in. Then make sure you actually do them once your targets have been met.*

▶ *Do your accounts early.*

11

Mobile working

In this chapter you will learn:

- **the advantages of increased flexibility**
- **how to minimize costs**
- **about 'virtual' businesses**
- **how to streamline your working practices**

'A self does not amount to much, but no self is an island;
each exists in a fabric of relations that is now more
complex and mobile than ever before.'

Jean-François Lyotard

Increased flexibility

One of the great advantages to being your own boss is the flexibility
you can take advantage of in your working life. We have already
looked at how you can use this to your advantage in the way in
which you structure your working week and your day-to-day routine,
but what if you need to stay in constant contact with suppliers, or
to ensure your clients have instant access to you no matter where
you are? Businesses are catering for an increasingly demanding
consumer base for whom deadlines are tighter and expectations
higher, driven by the growth of a service-based economy, and there
has never been greater pressure to respond quickly to clients, to
access information immediately and to maintain communication
continually. Fortunately in today's world of fast-paced, high-tech
information superhighways it is perfectly possible for the solo worker

to work anywhere they please, in any number of ways that suit them, because today's office packs up and fits neatly into a small holdall. Armed with a mobile phone, a Blackberry, an iPhone, a wireless connectivity laptop, a 3G dongle and a thermos of hot coffee we can go where the wind blows us, where we need to be or where we want to be. For many solo workers it makes little business sense to operate from a single office but rather to do business on the move to make the best use of their time and resources, and this peripatetic style of working is a growing trend. 'Management Futures', a report from the chartered management institute (CMI, 2008) concluded that developments in mobile working technology will increasingly enable the rise of 'virtual businesses' so that by 2018 a good deal of business will be completed through virtual contact alone, with efficient project management and the ability to work effectively from home two of the key skills workers will need to master.

SHAKING UP YOUR ROUTINE

If you need inspiration and your creative batteries are running low, or if you simply need a change of scene, being able to pack your office into your briefcase and leave your usual office space behind can provide a welcome relief and a much needed breath of fresh air – quite literally, if you so choose.

Case study

'I am a member of a club in town. This is a place with somewhere I can go to write or think as well as meet clients one-on-one for a chat or just a nice place to catch up with old colleagues (who have now gone solo themselves!) over lunch.'

Certainly many people find that one of the great pleasures of being their own boss is that they can, and do, throw everything they need into a bag and head off to a local coffee shop whenever they want to gain some perspective on the situation and where physically getting away from the office really helps, or when motivation is waning and just having other people around and being 'in public' will spur them on; or on a beautiful summer's day they swap the bag for a set of panniers and jump on their bicycle to combine work with exercise, a change of scene and a liberal dose of uplifting sunshine and fresh air.

Insight

Research has shown that 57 per cent of businesses offer mobile working to their employees in order to improve their work/life balance. As your own boss you are free to take advantage of this boon whenever – and wherever – you choose, so make the most of the advantages afforded by mobile working.

The ability to shake up your routine in this way not only makes working more pleasant, it can also help your business productivity. A survey from the Department of Business Enterprise and Regulatory Reform (BERR) found that 65 per cent of companies think that a flexible working routine improves staff motivation, with 50 per cent reporting increased productivity as a result. So if you feel like you need a change of scene then in all probability you really will benefit from the change, and so will your business.

EVER READY

No matter where you are, no matter where you are going, getting set up with the right equipment allows you to always be 'at the office'. This can be a great advantage for your clients, knowing that they can always reach you, no matter which time zone they are calling from or where you happen to be at the time. Providing an uninterrupted service in this way and appearing responsive at all times gives the impression of efficiency and professionalism which your clients will almost certainly expect. Furthermore, they will be reassured that when they do contact you you will be ready and able to converse on whatever it is they need to discuss since you will always have everything to hand. Perhaps they want to arrange a meeting or conference call, discuss a piece of research you sent them or walk you through a PowerPoint they have just sent you as an attachment to an email – whatever it is you will be able to get to it in a matter of minutes and your clients will be reassured knowing that you are always on hand to help them. It also gives you the reassurance that you will never miss that all-important call offering you some lucrative work.

YOUR COMPLETE PORTFOLIO

How many times have you gone to a meeting assuming you were fully prepared, only to discover that the client is also very interested in a completely different area, one which you deal with but not one for which you have resource material to hand. Of course you could always try to explain what it is you do and how you might be able to help them and you can promise faithfully to send them some examples as soon as you get back to the office but you will already have missed that golden moment, the one which offers you the very best opportunity to impress. How much better is it to be able to show your client precisely what it is you can do, right there and then, by showing them examples of similar projects you have already completed for other clients?

> **'If you are prepared, you will be confident, and will do the job.'**
>
> Tom Landry

Not only does mobile working allow you to seize the initiative, it ensures you can walk a client through your offer, explaining it to them first-hand and answering their questions. It also shows just how efficient and prepared you are, giving your clients (or prospective clients) confidence in your work and your working practices.

TURNING DEAD TIME INTO WORK TIME

As your own boss you will quickly discover that there are never enough hours in the day and one of the great frustrations is finding yourself with time to kill but not being able to use it efficiently.

This is a situation which happens all too often, whilst waiting for a meeting to start (you left extra early to give yourself plenty of time only for there to have been no traffic and now you have arrived at your destination with two hours to kill), at the airport waiting for your delayed flight to be called, in a soulless hotel room where some interesting work would prove a timely distraction and so on. Anything which seems to you to be a waste of time is therefore wasted time, and that is something you simply cannot afford, particularly in the early days of being your own boss.

> **'I do not want to waste any time. And if you are not working on important things, you are wasting time.'**
>
> Dean Kamen

Fortunately, by getting organized and setting yourself up with an efficient mobile working suite, the horrors of dead time can be not just minimized but eliminated altogether. The trick is to get into good habits: always make sure you take everything with you, all the time, wherever you go and for however long, whether or not you think there will be any need for them, or even if you absolutely know for certain that there won't be. That way, when the unexpected or even inconceivable happens, and you find yourself with time to kill you will be ready to take advantage of it.

Minimizing costs

Unless you are taking the leap to becoming your own boss because you have won the lottery and think it might prove an interesting diversion, then it is a fairly safe bet that you will want to minimize costs wherever possible. Although getting yourself set up with a fully flexible working arrangement will involve some not inconsiderable upfront costs it is an investment which can pay for itself in a very short space of time. For instance, if you want to keep yourself well organized and efficient (and why wouldn't you?) then you will need someone or something to organize your diary and field your calls. One option is to employ a personal assistant; another is to take advantage of today's technology and handle the task yourself. After all, you need only ever be a phone call or voicemail away and you will always have your diary with you. Need to book a flight or a venue for a meeting? No problem. At your fingertips you have the single best resource available to anyone, the world wide web, and you have the wherewithal to book whatever you need to book, and with some dextrous time management you can ensure you are filling one of those dread spots of otherwise dead time we have already looked at so it shouldn't even cause you unnecessary delay. The other side of the minimizing costs coin is revenue generation. If by having an efficient mobile working set-up you can win work you might otherwise have lost out on then that surely is the ultimate cost saving measure.

'Virtual' businesses

As your own boss in sole charge of your business, your company's profile is, to a large degree, whatever you want it to be. Or more accurately, whatever you decide it should be and therefore elect to project. You may work in a small study in your home, a converted bedroom or even a corner of the kitchen or a shed at the bottom of your garden, but unless your clients pay you a visit (and this is usually something to be avoided at all costs) then your offices are whatever picture you paint of them in your clients' minds.

Insight

Take a moment to picture your business as you would like it to be. Try to see it from all angles so that you build up a fully three-dimensional model, one which you can really see and believe in. Then commit it to memory so that whenever you talk about your business this is the image you convey.

Mobile working allows you to visit your clients which not only saves them the time and trouble of visiting you but also allows you to claim for the mileage! More importantly it enables you to create and maintain an image of your company which is the perfect reflection of the ideal situation – no matter how far from the truth it really is. If your clients ever want to meet up somewhere other than their offices (perhaps because they are going to be in your neck of the woods anyway and think they are doing you a favour) then your best bet is to rent a space for the purpose.

There are myriad versions on a theme available, from hiring a conference facility or a hotel venue to a serviced meeting room or simply an empty multipurpose space, so you shouldn't have too much difficulty in sourcing something which meets your needs. They also come in all shapes and sizes so you should be able to get something which is just right, impressing your clients while not forgetting to add the hire cost to your invoice, and all the while keeping secret the reality of your offices. After all, if the work you do is good what should it matter what your office space looks like?

Streamlining your working practices

It is a basic tenet of time/work management to try to ensure that you tackle several jobs of a roughly similar nature in one go, before moving on to another group of similar jobs and so on. A lot of time is wasted by flitting from one type of task to another to another as there is always a transition period required which is inevitably just dead time. Different pieces of equipment (hardware or software) may need to be removed and others put in their place; you will need to make the mental transition from one sort of task to another (often accompanied by a 'much-needed' break for a transitional cup of tea or coffee); information and documents may need to be located and relevant people contacted (e.g. accountant, legal adviser, suppliers or clients) so that you can establish pertinent facts and so on. This is especially true of small tasks where the transition period can often equal, and sometimes even outweigh the length of time required to complete the tasks themselves. Thus it follows that if you can get all your ducks in a row to begin with you can save yourself a lot of wasted time and effort and a good deal of needless frustration. Maximizing your workplace efficiency through disciplined organization is vital to the success of any solo worker.

> **'The highest type of efficiency is that which can utilize existing material to the best advantage.'**
>
> Jawaharlal Nehru

The best way to go about this is to identify which tasks can readily be combined into groups of a similar nature, and how often such tasks need to be completed, which can wait and which are urgent etc. Then identify the optimal number of tasks which can be completed in one session. Obviously this will depend on the nature and type of each task or group of tasks, and it is likely that no two groups will be exactly the same so try to establish the rules for each group individually. By knowing the length of time required to complete each task and the frequency at which the tasks occur you can plan ahead to ensure they are completed in a timely manner. Moreover, by sorting them into relevant work groups you will ensure they are completed in manageable sections, not piecemeal nor randomly, making them easier to deal with as well as more efficient. So capitalize on the flexibility provided by mobile working to ensure that no matter where you are and regardless of the project or projects on which you are currently employed you have to hand every single piece of work you need to complete so that you can always work on a logical group of work pieces in one go. By eliminating the need to cherry-pick your work and the sequence in which it is completed you will streamline your working practices making you more efficient and more effective.

KEY THINGS TO REMEMBER

▶ *Exploiting mobile-working technologies affords the solo worker an unprecedented level of workplace flexibility.*

▶ *The ability to remain in constant contact with clients, suppliers etc. gives them the reassurance that you are always to hand.*

▶ *The capacity to stay in touch with your business no matter where in the world you are creates a freedom you can and should exploit in your working life.*

▶ *Taking advantage of being your own boss and not needing to remain in the office all the time affords you the opportunity to shake up your routine once in a while.*

▶ *Be prepared. By having your complete portfolio of past, present and future work always to hand you can ensure you are always ready to seize an opportunity when it occurs.*

▶ *Turn any would-be down-time into an unexpected and valuable opportunity to work on current projects or to begin fishing for new ones.*

▶ *Capitalize on your ability to keep costs to a minimum by utilizing the benefits of mobile working.*

▶ *Visualize your business as you want others to see it and use that template to paint for them a picture of your company.*

▶ *Streamline your working practices by ensuring that you always have to hand every piece of work which needs to be completed enabling you to group them efficiently and deal with them effectively.*

12

Working 5 to 9

In this chapter you will learn:
- *about 5-to-9 working and how to make it work for you*
- *about the enterprise renaissance*
- *whether your hobby could be turned into a successful business*

What is 5-to-9 working?

Over the past decade, and particularly in the last three to four years, there has been a sharp increase in the number of people who are combining paid employment in a full- or part-time job with running their own company in their spare time, earning some extra income from doing something they really want to do. This is 5-to-9 working (working from 5 p.m. to 9 p.m.). The major benefit is that it allows people who want to become their own boss full time to start with baby steps, trying out their ideas and establishing and growing their business while enjoying the safety and security of knowing that they do not need to rely on its profits for their livelihood. This safety net encourages people who might not otherwise take the leap to solo working to have a go at running their own business, and for many not having the pressure of needing to have a viable business generating income from day one allows them the freedom to experiment in order to get their offer absolutely right. The biggest downside is the number of hours which need to be worked and the subsequent decrease in the time available to relax and to spend with family and friends.

'There's nothing like biting off more than you can chew, and then chewing anyway.'

Mark Burnett

Indeed, many 5-to-9 workers cite the loss of a social life as being one of the biggest drawbacks; another is that they cannot devote 100 per cent of their time to their business. If you can make it work for you, however, then this is a great way to start your business slowly, allowing you to try it out before you commit to making it your full-time job and your only source of income.

A GROWING TREND

Driven by fears about the economy, the possibility of redundancy, and the perceived difficulties of securing start-up bank loans for a full-time business without that business having a proven track record, an increasing number of entrepreneurs are deciding to set up and run their own company in their spare time, whilst remaining in full-time or part-time employment. The potential offered by the latest technology is another important factor, particularly the widespread uptake of electronic communications which mean that opening hours are not an issue – orders can be placed any time of the day or night and from anywhere in the world, and actioned the next time the 5-to-9er opens for business. This method of trading is already widespread with a significant number of people starting their businesses in this way and it is a large and steadily growing trend. A recent survey by home business website Enterprise Nation discovered that more than 5 million people in the UK are currently earning some form of income from home and that of the businesses being run part time, 50 per cent are steadily growing. They also state that, according to online auctioneers eBay, the number of Britons with a full-time or hobby eBay business grew some 160 per cent to 178,000 between 2006 and 2008, and that freelancing website www.peopleperhour.com estimates that about a third of all new registrations are from 5-to-9ers. Personal assistant providers www.moneypenny.co.uk, meanwhile, estimate that approximately three in ten calls to their business are from people with a full-time job who run a business on the side, a figure which increases to six in ten calls if you include part-time workers and husband/wife groups. And it is a trend which shows no signs of slowing down – indeed with an increasing rollout and uptake of communication technologies, particularly broadband internet connectivity, and a growing awareness of the possibilities of making a living from an erstwhile hobby, the number of people working 5 to 9 is likely to continue to increase. This will be further fuelled by the introduction of recent legislation in the UK enabling parents of children aged 16 and under (approximately 4.5 million people) greater rights to request flexible and part-time working hours, enabling them to start a home-based business.

The enterprise renaissance

For some people the thrill of running their own business is reward enough, and they enjoy the lack of pressure which results from not needing it to be sufficiently successful that it can support them financially. For the overwhelming majority of 5-to-9ers, however, the intention is to turn it into a full-time business as soon as it has gained sufficient momentum.

'The difference between try and triumph is a little umph.'

(author unknown)

The advantage of launching their company while remaining in paid employment is that it provides them with a safe route to giving up their day job, with a built-in fallback plan, but most 5-to-9ers set out with a very clear idea of when they expect their business to be able to support them. According to the *Sunday Times* newspaper, two-thirds hope their part-time businesses will be sufficiently profitable to enable them to quit work and run them full-time within one year and for the majority reaching the tipping point which will allow them to give up their paid employ cannot come soon enough. In the meantime these spare-room, spare-time start-ups enjoy the luxury of establishing their businesses in relative safety and as their business grows so does their confidence (and their bank balance) as they count down the days until they feel able to make the leap to becoming their own boss – at a time of their own choosing.

Making 5-to-9 working work for you

If the idea of becoming your own boss in your own time is appealing, perhaps to enable you and your business to gain a foothold before committing to becoming your own boss full-time, then why not join the millions of people who are already enjoying extra income from working 5 to 9? All the same rules apply as if you were taking the leap to becoming your own boss full time straightaway, but you will face one additional challenge – how to maintain a social life (and find enough time to sleep!) while devoting all your spare time to working. Do not underestimate just how many hours you might have to put in in the evenings and weekends to get your business off the ground. Indeed many 5-to-9 workers estimate that they put in as many hours (if not more) on their 'part-time' business as they do on their full-time job!

> **'Hard work spotlights the character of people: some turn up their sleeves, some turn up their noses, and some don't turn up at all.'**
>
> Sam Ewing

If you are prepared to put in the long hours and the hard work then working 5 to 9 can be a great way to get started as your own boss. One word of caution though – there are any number of guides to part-time working which suggest possible business opportunities you might like to consider, such as private tutoring, life coaching, catering, virtual PA etc., if you like the idea of becoming a 5-to-9er but you are unclear on the direction your business should take. While these can provide useful food for thought you will need to bear in mind that if you are in need of advice as to the type of company you should start, what your offer should be and the nature of the work you should do, then you may not be sufficiently prepared to launch your own company – or sufficiently passionate about your new business to make it successful. So if you find yourself reading through such lists, cherry-picking career options to draw up a shortlist which appeals to you, then it is time for some rigorous soul-searching as to your reasons for wanting to become a 5-to-9er and what you hope to gain from your business.

Insight

Casting about for business ideas suggests that you do not have a clear vision for your business and a burning desire to create an offer around something about which you are passionate. If this is the case are you really prepared to put in the long hours required of any successful 5-to-9er, to give up a good part of your social life and to persevere when the going gets tough?

Imagine coming home after a long day at work and straight away settling yourself in your office to put in another six or seven hours of work, then at the weekend working 9 to 5 on your part-time business and quite possibly working 5 to 9 as well. If you are not truly passionate about your new business then putting in the hours and covering the hard yards will seem very hard indeed.

'When I was young, I observed that nine out of ten things I did were failures. So I did ten times more work.'

George Bernard Shaw

Lucrative hobby or the foundation of a successful business?

Starting your business by working 5 to 9 can be particularly valuable if you are unsure of the commercial credentials of the product or service you intend to supply. Quitting your job to run your company full time before you are even sure there is a marketplace for your offer makes poor business sense, but doing so part time allows you to test your business in a low-risk way. With the financial security your day job affords you are free to test your offer on the open market and very soon you will get a good idea of its commercial viability. You need to use this time to assess rigorously whether or not your idea needs to remain a pipe dream, or whether it really can become a profitable business. You will need to be brutally honest with yourself which is far easier said than done. Your business idea may be a long-held dream, something which you have for a long time been thinking about doing and in which you may well have already invested a good deal – of time, hope, ambition, emotion and money.

▶ *If all the indications are that your idea is* not commercially viable *then you need to be honest with yourself about your findings. It is painful to have your business dreams shattered in this way but far more painful to ignore the warning signs and give up your day job only to have brutally demonstrated to you what you already knew. If you really enjoy doing whatever it is you do as a 5-to-9er then why not continue with it as an enjoyable hobby from which you make some money? Alternatively you can reassess your business proposition, further research the market place to fully understand why your idea was not met with the same enthusiasm as you hoped it would be and finetune or reposition your offer as required, or even go back to the drawing board and start again.*
▶ *If all the indications are that your idea is* commercially viable *and you have proof that people are willing to pay a sufficient price for your product or service that you can generate a decent profit, and provided that your research shows that the market and your potential share of it is large enough to make it worth your while, then you can quickly assess the risk involved in giving up your job to run the business full time. If all the indications are that your new business can be sufficiently profitable to meet your needs then it is all systems go and you will be able to give up your job and commit yourself fully to your new enterprise with the reassurance that you are not going into it blind but that you have rigorously tested your idea in the marketplace first.*

It is however important to remember that often the more you do the more you want to do, and that once you are concentrating solely on your erstwhile 5-to-9 business you may find your drive beginning to wane.

Insight

Be prepared that if you give up your paid employment and make your erstwhile 5-to-9 business your full-time job you will immediately face all the challenges, as well as all the opportunities, set out in this book.

So before you make the transition, ensure that you are mentally prepared for the reality that as soon as you only have one job on which to concentrate you can all too easily lose the focus which has made your business the success it is. You should, of course, enjoy the new-found freedom which comes with being your own boss full time, but not at the expense of continuing to put in the hard work needed to grow your business.

'Most of us can easily do two things at once; what's all but impossible is to do one thing at once.'

Mignon McLaughlin

KEY THINGS TO REMEMBER

▶ *Starting a business in your spare time while remaining in paid employment can provide a useful stepping stone to launching a new career.*

▶ *Working 5 to 9 affords you the luxury of establishing your businesses in relative safety – as your business grows so will your confidence and your bank balance.*

▶ *Do not underestimate the amount of work required – you will need to be prepared to work long into the evenings and at weekends.*

▶ *Remember that by working 5 to 9 you will not be able to devote yourself entirely to your new enterprise.*

▶ *You will need to be prepared to lose a good deal of your social life as well as a good deal of sleep!*

▶ *Working 5 to 9 is a growing trend with an increasing number of people and companies offering support if you choose to take this route.*

▶ *Working 5 to 9 is an excellent and relatively low-risk way of testing your offer in the marketplace.*

▶ *If you decide to quit your job to focus on your company full time, be prepared to continue working long into the evenings and at weekends, at least in the early stages, to enable your business to grow sufficiently to support you.*

13

IT for the solo worker

In this chapter you will learn:
- *how information technology can enhance your business*
- *about current technologies of comunication and connectivity*

'Information technology and business are becoming inextricably interwoven. I don't think anybody can talk meaningfully about one without talking about the other.'

Bill Gates

Information technology and the technologies of communication and connectivity may be something which inspires and excites you or it may make your blood run cold; perhaps it is something with which you are already familiar and a suite of high-tech devices already adorns your office, or perhaps you have yet to succumb to the terrors of mobile phones and broadband internet access, wireless connectivity and dongles, Blackberries, Skypeing, IM etc. Either way, it is something which your clients are likely to expect and even demand of you and, as we have already seen, it is something which can boost your productivity as well as your efficiency and help to project an image of accessibility and professionalism. We are truly in the age of instant access instant response, 24/7 zero-downtime connectivity which, used appropriately, can provide a lifeline to you and your business. A failure to embrace the information technology which allows this degree of flexibility, however, is to shoot yourself in the foot from a business perspective before you have even got your company up and running, so if you feel uneasy about the IT side of your business it is time to bite the bullet! The necessary technologies can be broken down into four main areas: information, communication, connectivity and data management.

Information

Thanks to the internet there has never been an easier time to research and gather information. By accessing the world wide web, be it from a computer in the office, a wireless enabled laptop in a 'hotspot' (an area which provides remote internet access, often free of charge) or from a mobile phone or similar device with sufficiently fast data download capability (usually 3G or better) we can instantly plug into a world of information accessed through powerful and increasingly accurate search engines (such as Google, Yahoo, Ask etc.), with the world's largest and surely most comprehensive encyclopaedia, Wikipedia, never more than a few clicks away (just bear in mind that as content is uploaded by users all around the world it is open to a degree of inaccuracy, although by and large it tends to be pretty good). Having such a rich resource constantly at your disposal is truly wonderful and can certainly save an awful lot of time when compared to the methods of choice previously at our disposal such as cumbersome (and limited) encyclopaedia or bouncing from one phone call to the next trying to get closer and closer to finding someone with the elusive information, telephone number, reference etc. for which we were searching. One word of caution – the world wide web can be dangerously addictive and 'surfing' (skipping contentedly from one website to another tangential and equally tempting site, or on to a different type of site altogether sparked by a reference or recommendation) can cost countless working hours if you are not wise to the risk and careful to be very disciplined.

> **'Anyone who has lost track of time when using a computer knows the propensity to dream, the urge to make dreams come true and the tendency to miss lunch.'**
>
> Tim Berners-Lee

There is a good reason why most companies restrict their employees' internet access at work and block the use of certain sites. As soon as you are your own boss you will enjoy the freedom of unlimited internet access so it is up to you to be sufficiently self-disciplined to define and implement your own internet rules of engagement.

> **Insight**
>
> The world wide web – one of the most valuable and productive resources available to you and your business, and one of the most addictive, alluring and potentially dangerous.

Communication

Like it or not we are in the age of continuous and never-ending contact, and this is something which is increasingly being expected and demanded by clients, customers, suppliers and even colleagues. A mobile phone is the first step and – good news for those who shrink from the prospect of getting to grips with a whole raft of new technology – in many cases it can prove to be the only necessary piece of communication equipment. Having a dedicated telephone landline, or at least a dedicated landline number for your business, is also an option and can help to make your business look better and bigger (useful if you want people to imagine your business is a large and thriving enterprise situated in a big and busy office block) but you will still need to get a mobile phone and get into the habit of answering it in your best business voice every time it rings if the display is not telling you it is one of your friends or family members on the line. Make sure you set up your voicemail to best advantage too. If you do not record your own message it will revert to the default setting, an impersonal and generic greeting leaving any potential customer wondering whether they got the right number and whether you ever got their message. It is also an opportunity wasted – first impressions count and if this is a client's first contact with you and with your company then it is a golden opportunity to greet them in a professional manner, with a message recorded by you, which reflects the personality of your company. If the nature of your business is such that it is likely you will receive a lot of telephone calls from customers (and potential customers) and if you tend to spend a fair amount of time on your mobile chatting to friends then it may be worth investing in a mobile phone dedicated to your business, a phone to which you give priority. It is perfectly acceptable to expect customers to leave the odd message because you are busy (presumably helping other customers) and not always available to answer the phone, but if this becomes the rule rather than the exception then it can be off-putting and the last thing you need when trying to establish your business is to risk losing customers or clients because you are enjoying your new-found freedom as your own boss by chatting to friends during business hours.

Case study

'When I first went freelance I was so excited and found it so liberating to be my own boss, making my own rules and setting my own standards, that I took far too many liberties although at the time I didn't really realize it. The opportunity to phone my friends whenever I wanted to, for instance, was far too tempting to ignore! Also, they knew about my new-found freedom, and now that I had left my employer where taking social calls during business hours was a strict no-no, they were free to phone me whenever they wanted to. At first it was wonderful until I took stock of my situation after the first month and realized that I hadn't achieved nearly as much as I had expected to. Not only was I spending too much time on the phone but, more damaging to my business, potential clients were being put off by the way I was never available. Of course I only realized this with hindsight and made moves immediately to remedy the situation – including risking hurting my friends by telling them they could no longer call me during office hours. Fortunately for me they were great about it and now we joke that they almost cost me my business, but if I hadn't acted to remedy the situation when I did, and as drastically as I did, it wouldn't have been so funny.'

Connectivity

Keeping in touch with your business, your suppliers and your client base is crucial to keeping track of demands and staying one step ahead of the game. We have looked at communication as a separate topic even though it could be broadly grouped under the heading of 'Connectivity' because it is such a vital and wide-ranging area. Connectivity in a larger sense, then, is all the other methods we have at our disposal for keeping connected to our working life whenever and wherever we may happen to be and allowing, indeed encouraging, our customers to keep connected to our business at all times. Facilitating this is fundamentally important to fostering a good and long-lasting relationship. It is when customers connect with your business of their own accord, voluntarily and without any stimulus from you, that real and lasting connections are made.

> **'Communication – the human connection – is the key to personal and career success.'**
>
> Paul Meyer

Your job is to ensure you have provided sufficient tools to enable this to happen and made them sufficiently accessible and user-friendly that they are easy and enjoyable to use. You will also need to make sure that everyone knows about them and that they are kept relevant through regular updates. Depending on your type of business and client base it may not be necessary or even advantageous to have more than one connectivity tool in use, but however many you feel is appropriate, try to employ only those which reflect your business' personality. With the number of different methods available today we are spoilt for choice, with a wide range of styles and varying degrees of technical expertise required by the user. As a general rule it is better to have only one very well designed and targeted tool than to try to cover all bases and overstretch yourself. It is tempting to want to encompass them all, partly because your business is new and exciting and you want it to have everything and arrive with a bang declaring itself proudly to the world, partly because you feel that without utilizing every tool at your disposal you are missing out and this might reflect badly on your company as well as resulting in you missing out on some lucrative work, and partly because you are unsure which tools will prove most useful and which your customers would want given the choice. By looking at it from the perspective of what your company provides, the image of it that you wish to project, and the demographic of your core clients you can get a clearer idea of where you should focus your time and resources, both of which may well be stretched in the early days of your new business' life. Do not forget that you can always add more at a future date, and even take offline any which are not working for your business – and you may not get it right first time so get into the habit of monitoring the usage of any connectivity tools in which you invest and ask customers if they have tried them yet and if so what did they think.

Insight

In order to get the most useful feedback from your clients on your connectivity tools try to structure your questions in an open manner so that you gain real insight. Do not just ask them if they thought the tools were good or not – ask questions such as what were their favourite and least favourite aspects of the tools, which they used for longest and why, and what they would like to see in the future.

Let's take a look at some of the more commonly employed connectivity tools businesses use to keep in touch with their customers and clients:

WEBSITE

The most obvious and almost certainly the most necessary connectivity tool is a website and it is very likely that this will be the first one you employ. Unfortunately this is unlikely to be the simplest and most straightforward option, nor the cheapest, but as a connectivity tool for your business it is unparalleled. A good website will reflect the personality and values of your business, communicate exactly what it is you offer and what your company can do for potential clients, provide a range of real-life examples coupled with quotes from satisfied (or preferably delighted) clients and list all your contact details. Depending on the nature of your business you might also provide an idea of timescale and cost for jobs. You can upload some carefully selected photos into your site which not only break up the pages and make the site easier and more enjoyable to navigate but can also communicate a good deal about your offer. You might include links to other websites which support your business proposition, directly or indirectly, and you might even have a resource section on your website which can be accessed by anyone visiting your site, or can be password protected so that it is accessible only to existing clients. You might even decide to make this area accessible to anyone who is willing to part with their contact details allowing you to directly target people you know to be interested in your offer. Whatever you decide to include, try to ensure your site remains easily navigable and clutter-free.

> **'Web users ultimately want to get at data quickly and easily. They don't care as much about attractive sites and pretty design.'**
>
> Tim Berners-Lee

By detailing all your contact information, potential clients have all the details they need to get in touch with you at their leisure, and can even send you an email just by clicking on a link – thereby turning passive connectivity into active communication and with any luck establishing a relationship from which you can gain some business. Of course you do not need to have everything on your website from day one (indeed you are unlikely to be able to get everything from the outset, such as the necessary references to fill the 'what our customers say about us' quotes section) and trying to do so may prove inhibitive, either in terms of financial cost if you are employing someone to create your website for you, or in terms of time cost if you are going to do it all yourself. That does not matter, it can grow and evolve over time. What definitely does matter is that your website is of a quality that reflects your business and your ambitions for your business. It is far better to have a simple website which looks and feels of a very high quality, even if it only sports a little about what your business does and who and how you can help, together with your contact details, than to have a large but messy website of dubious quality and poor design which will have potential clients questioning your ability to provide good service before you have even had a chance to make contact with them personally and impress them. It has been said that if a passenger on an aircraft sees so much as a coffee stain on their flip-down tray they will start to wonder if the engines have been properly serviced. In the same way a poor website can undermine your entire business and deter potential clients. After all, if you cannot provide a decent website then what is the likelihood that you can provide a decent business service? So build your website one piece at a time, making sure that every iteration oozes quality and clearly reflects your company's personality and values.

BLOG

Another option you may wish to consider is a blog. This is simply an online spiel about whatever you want it to be about – updates about your company, musings on the state of the industry, thoughts on the latest trends or reviews of anything you might use in your business. Quite simply, there are blogs about anything and everything. The key, so often ignored, is to keep your blog focused and regularly updated. All too often a well-meaning business blogger gets sidetracked and either starts to discuss something of interest to them but unconnected to their business (and so unlikely to be of interest to their readers) or to use their virtual soapbox to rant and rave and generally vent their spleen about any number of ills which ail their business and patently are not their fault! Others use it as a virtual pulpit from which to preach worthily about business matters or just life in general, all of which might make them feel better but are unlikely to do much to boost their business. So try to keep your blog focused on your business – it can be useful to get someone else to review it from time to time to make sure that it stays on track.

By updating your blog regularly you ensure that the content is always topical and relevant, and you provide a reason for your customers to visit your site on a regular basis, so try to get into the habit of updating your blog at least once per week, and updating it on the same day (or days) each week. This also ensures that your website looks modern and cared for and your business appears up to date and together. If you visit a website with a blog which has not been updated for weeks (or months or years) it does not fill you with confidence about the company. So, if you are going to blog then make sure that you blog regularly and ensure that your topic is one about which you are passionate and have plenty to say.

Insight

It is better not to blog at all than to blog poorly, and once you have started a blog it may damage your company's image if it is not updated regularly or if it suddenly disappears altogether.

TWITTER

This is a form of mini blog used mainly for social commentary but it can be a useful way of keeping people updated on a very regular basis. It is free of charge to use but you will need to update it ever so frequently (preferably at least once a day) in order to keep it relevant, which is not only time-consuming but requires that your subject has no end of talking points which your potential audience will find interesting and stimulating. In a business context, twittering is perhaps useful only if you need to maintain a constant connection with your clients to keep your business permanently front of mind and it will need to be in a tone and style which is entertaining. In other words, you need to give your customers a reason to want to keep checking back.

Insight

Beware – twittering (or 'tweeting') can be a great way of keeping clients posted on all your business activities, but it is very high maintenance and can quickly become more trouble than it is worth, so before you begin you will need to be clear about your reasons for wanting to maintain such regular contact.

FACEBOOK

Many companies are now turning to Facebook as a method of communicating with their audience. One of the advantages this affords is that the communication is two-way, enabling visitors to keep updated with the latest information on your company and your offer while at the same time providing them with the means of contacting you to provide feedback, ask questions and so on. Another is that it is free of charge! A further string to Facebook's bow is that it is primarily a social networking medium so a company's page can leverage this equity – visitors are likely to be less guarded and less sceptical when reading a Facebook page than when visiting a company's website.

YOUTUBE

This hugely popular video broadcast website is a great way to provide video content to your clients. A simple link on your website can connect them straight to this material with the added benefit that YouTube users might enjoy your videos and then search out your website on the internet. The main point to consider here is whether or not you have any material which is best suited to this form of communication – if it would be better served just by being on your website then you should limit it to that.

VIRAL GAMES AND IPHONE APPS

Simple viral games and apps for iPhone, iPad, Ovi etc. can be a great way to keep your company or product front of mind for your clients, while providing them with a genuine reason for wanting to maintain a connection with you, namely entertainment. The two barriers to this method of connectivity are cost and time. Depending on the scale and quality of your product this may take too long to achieve or be too costly to implement, at least in the initial stages of your business growth. You will also need to determine whether or not engaging your customers in this way is right for your business.

Data management

There are, of course, myriad ways to store data but the crucial aspect is to ensure you have a ready-made backup of everything you have on your hard drive so that you never find yourself in the business-stalling situation of a mid-project data loss. Unless you are in a position to go straight into having a server (and most start-up businesses are not) then an external hard drive is the answer. Fortunately these are now fairly cheap for even very sizeable hard drives and most come with a basic dedicated software package to make backing up your data a simple and quick process. Many will even have an automatic backup feature, allowing the external hard drive to access and copy all the selected data from your PC or Apple automatically at pre-determined intervals defined by the user, ensuring you never need to remember to do it manually – a lifesaver for most busy business owners busy being their own boss. Either way, you need to ensure that your external hard drive is backed up very frequently; it is, after all, only ever as up to date as you let it be and an out-of-date backup is of limited value. So, set up your external hard drive to automatically back up your data at frequent intervals or make sure you are ultra-disciplined in doing so yourself.

Insight

A complete copy of the latest state of your hard drive really is one of those things you never fully appreciate until you need it. Only then do you discover its true value.

The minimum requirement

The extent to which you will need to be always accessible to your clients, and the degree to which you will need to have an unending capability to access them, your diary, your other business contacts, suppliers, the world wide web etc. will of course depend on the nature and profile of your new business and your vision for it, as well as a realistic determination of the optimum way to achieve this, but for almost everyone going solo and becoming their own boss there is a minimum requirement of information technology which will need to be embraced. Let us suppose, quite reasonably, that your new business venture will require you to be in contact with the outside world, and that you want to ensure you do not needlessly miss out on valuable work. Let us suppose too that you want to convey an image of being efficient and having your act together and not being stuck in the dark ages. If all of this is true of you and your business, then the minimum requirement which can reasonably be expected is that you have a dedicated business telephone line and answering service of some variety to field calls and take messages in your absence, and a business email address.

If reading this you are breaking into a cold sweat and retreating in denial then you are not alone. It is constantly amazing just how many people devote a great deal of time, money and effort, to say nothing of their hopes and dreams and ambitions, to setting up and launching their new business and yet refuse point blank to get themselves and their business set up with even the minimum IT infrastructure, in some cases not even a mobile phone or email address! And such unwillingness to embrace modern information technology is certainly not limited to those who are launching a new business because they have retired – it is a reluctance demonstrated by certain people of all ages and with all types of businesses.

Insight

Anyone who refuses to embrace information technology or anything else which might abet their business, no matter how much they might personally dislike it or feel intimidated by it, needs to think very carefully about just how serious they are about their business and their business ambitions. Not only might you be missing out on valuable work but you will almost certainly be inconveniencing your customers. It is also a clear signal of not being prepared to throw yourself into your new career with as much gusto as you might – which is to say completely, utterly and wholeheartedly.

KEY THINGS TO REMEMBER

▶ Whether you are excited by information technology or left cold by it, you cannot afford to ignore it.

▶ Learn to use the internet efficiently and effectively and you will always have at your disposal what must surely be the greatest information resource ever created.

▶ The communication infrastructure modern technology allows – provided you are willing to embrace it – means you need never miss out on a single piece of work.

▶ Be careful not to let the new found freedom of being your own boss and the never-ending connectivity provided by modern IT tempt you to spend your working life socializing.

▶ Take the time to explore the pros and cons of the many connectivity tools at your disposal and execute only those you think will provide a significant and tangible benefit to your business.

▶ At the very least ensure your business has an excellent website – clean, clear and easy to navigate with a minimum of information, all of which is entirely relevant to your company and of genuine use to your clients.

▶ If you think it may be beneficial to your business to blog and/or twitter make sure that you have enough relevant and interesting material to sustain them.

▶ Make sure you have thought through the cost implications (including long-term maintenance and updates) before committing to any viral games and/or iPhone apps etc.

▶ Make sure you always have at least one up-to-date backup of your hard drive(s).

▶ Your clients have the right to expect you to have embraced at least the minimum of information technology tools – and they will.

14

Accounting for successful business

In this chapter you will learn:
- **about different trading methods**
- **about your company's books and whether you need an accountant**
- **about insurance, sources of funding and purchase tax**

It is never too early to start

'The very best financial presentation is one that's well thought out and anticipates any questions ... answering them in advance.'

Nathan Collins

Getting your new business' finances in order is one of the most important tasks you face when you become your own boss and it is never too early to start – indeed several elements can and should be completed *before* you quit your old job. We have already seen how important it is to have your company bank account set up from day one, but it is just as important to have established a sound financial framework for your business so that you really can hit the ground running. You will need to think ahead for each month, quarter and year, trying to estimate the likely running costs of your business and map these against your profit forecast for the business, and you will need to keep a close eye on your accounts to see if things are panning out as you had anticipated and what corrections, if any, you need to implement to ensure your business is profitable. In the early days of your business' life it can be difficult to predict your incomings and outgoings accurately, but don't let this deter you from putting in place a broad finance structure which can be adjusted as necessary as you go along.

'If you have to forecast, forecast often.'

Edgar R. Fiedler

So what are the key elements of your business finances you need to have thought through, decided upon and set up, and what is the timescale for each?

BEFORE YOU QUIT YOUR JOB

In order to be able to make the most of your new business from your very first day of trading you will need to have certain things in place before you begin. We have already looked at the need to have a business bank account so that you can keep your personal and business accounts separate from the outset and so that you can begin to invoice clients. It can take a little while to set this up so make sure you begin the process well ahead of quitting your job and be clear as to what you require of your business bank account. If you simply need it as a repository for your company's funds then a basic business account will be sufficient to your needs and the majority of banks will be more than happy to accept your custom.

Insight

Be sure to shop around as each will have in place a different cost structure, some offering incentives such as free processing of cheques or a certain number of complimentary electronic fund transfers per year, but these might come at a cost, e.g. needing to ensure the funds in your account never fall below a certain minimum level or being required to deposit a minimum amount into your account every month.

Make sure you think about the nature of your business, particularly with regards to its cash flow, before making your choice. If you expect to receive a large quantity of cheques and your income stream to be regular, constant and predictable then an account which requires regular deposits or a minimum reserve of funds might be suitable. If on the other hand your business is likely to generate larger sums of money but from just a few clients once or twice per year, then this sort of account is unlikely to prove cost-effective. Many banks also offer an inducement to starting your business banking with them in the form of an initial cost-free period, sometimes as long as two years, and unlike the majority of personal accounts, business accounts generally incur a monthly or quarterly fee, often with the addition of extra costs for any services used in that period, so free banking can be a real benefit, especially in the early stages of the life of your new business. Do bear in mind however that once this time has elapsed your bank will start to charge you, so make sure that you do not commit yourself for the long term to any account which may become very expensive once the initial honeymoon period is over. Most accounts will also offer extra services such as company credit cards (which your bank will be very keen for you to accept), but although these can be tempting be careful not to let your excitement get the better of you and to weigh up very carefully the pros and cons of using them as this will incur additional fees which can be quite expensive. Do they genuinely service the needs of your business or are you tempted to get one just for convenience? Is there a better way to pay for the goods and services your business requires? Are you tempted to get a company credit card because it will make you feel good to have one?

Insight

If you have been planning the move to becoming your own boss for a long time you might well have anticipated the thrill of being able to hand over a company credit card every time you charge legitimate business expenses to your company, but remember that if you don't really need a credit card for your business then you're better off doing without.

You will also need to have arranged sufficient initial capital to get your business up and running. In order to determine how much this needs to be it is a good rule of thumb to think through all your initial business requirements including the cost of one-off or irregular purchases such as IT equipment, vehicles, specialized plant or equipment etc. and any ongoing expenses such as office rental, heating and lighting, telephone bills etc., sufficient to see you through the first nine months of trading. Then double it. It is very rare to find someone who becomes their own boss and sets up their own company only to find that everything is much cheaper than they had anticipated!

ONCE YOU HAVE BECOME YOUR OWN BOSS

In addition to your initial capital, the expenses you predict your business will incur in set-up costs, you will also need some working capital and a contingency fund. The working capital is the amount of money your business needs to keep it running smoothly week by week. For some companies this can be just a few hundred pounds while for others it can be tens of thousands; what it is for your company will depend on the nature of your business and your plans for its development and expansion, but it is vital that you ensure your cash flow never haemorrhages. Because accurately forecasting your company's cash flow requirements is prone to so many errors, particularly when you first set up your business, it is wise to put in place a contingency fund, money which is always kept readily available but which is only ever used in cases of financial emergencies. You should always aim to keep your business accounts and your personal accounts completely separate, of course, and having a contingency fund will help to ensure that you do not need to dip into your personal savings to shore up your business in hard times. For accounting purposes it is vital that they are not allowed to merge but in practical terms, although it is not advisable, it is feasible to allow one to borrow from the other. You should of course always try to avoid this, not least because it is nearly always the business account which borrows from the personal account, not the other way around, but in practice it can often be difficult to achieve. The bottom line is that if your company bank account shows your company to be insolvent and lacking the funds necessary to continue trading, but you are convinced that this is only a temporary setback and very soon your company will be generating a handsome profit, then you will almost certainly be tempted to lend your company the necessary funds. If this is the case it is important to remember three things:

▶ *Despite your best efforts to forecast the financial requirements of your business, something has gone badly awry. You will need to determine why this is so in order to try to prevent it from happening again and also to ensure you identify any flaws in your business strategy.*

▶ *Make sure you really have only* loaned *your company the money and that you do get it back. Put a realistic timescale in place for this to happen and remember that it doesn't matter how well everything seems to be going and how much you manage to convince yourself that your company is the success you hoped and anticipated it would be, until your business is able to repay you it is insolvent.*

▶ *In a worst-case scenario you may be forced to ask your bank for a short-term loan. If this is the case, be very sure that you have a repayment vehicle in place for your company before you initiate the borrowing and that you have accounted for the extra costs your company will incur as a result of the interest charges. Also make sure that you get any promises of short-term funding in writing at the earliest opportunity to prevent any potentially damaging misunderstandings or confusion at a later date.*

'If you want to give a man credit, put it in writing. If you want to give him hell, do it on the phone.'

Charles Beacham

Different trading methods

When you become your own boss there are several different trading mediums you can employ and each has their own unique benefits and drawbacks. You will need to decide which method is best suited to your needs and the needs of your company, taking into account such factors as the level of risk, the degree of capital investment required, the financial implications of paying corporate tax versus personal tax and so on. Make sure that you determine the implications to you and your business of each different method over the short, medium and long term before committing yourself. Most accountants will be happy to model each trading method according to your projection for your business to help you to determine which one is most likely to work best for you and your company financially so that you can make an informed decision, but remember that this is only part of the equation. The good news is that there are really only two options you need to consider unless there will be several people jointly owning and running the business (in which case a partnership might be preferable) or you think that floating your company on the stock market as a PLC from day one is going to be viable!

SOLE TRADER

This is the technical term for being self-employed and it is the simplest label under which to start your business. The biggest drawback to being a sole trader is that you are personally liable for all your business debts, something which is obviously not to be taken lightly – if the worst-case scenario were to occur and your business were to go bankrupt leaving massive unpaid debts, as a sole trader you could have to sell your house as well as any other capital assets in order to pay your creditors. This is because there is no legal difference between the money belonging to your business or to you personally (although you will still need to keep your personal and business book-keeping separate). If, however, your business requires you to take few risks and to own few capital assets then this might be your simplest and easiest option.

LIMITED COMPANY

The biggest advantage of this method of trading is that it protects your personal property should your company go bankrupt.

You will of course lose all the company's assets and any shares you hold in the business will be rendered worthless, but unless you have committed any personal assets in order to secure funding (e.g. to a bank or building society) you can rest assured that at the very least your home is not at risk. On the downside you may find an accountant will charge more if your company is incorporated than if you are a sole trader and there is more paperwork and bureaucracy to deal with. Also bear in mind that while it is easy to form a limited company it can be complicated to close it down.

Your company's books

Keeping your company's accounts accurate and up to date is a housekeeping chore most of us will willingly put off for as long as we possibly can before forcing our way through them with gritted teeth and an air of despondency. They are however a necessary evil, and keeping on top of them on a regular basis is a lot less hassle in the long run than not keeping on top of them. They are vital to your company's success, not only to ensure you always pay the correct amount of tax (a task which you simply *have* to get right every time) but also if they are to act as a yardstick to the profitability of your business. Simply put, an accurate, up-to-date and easy-to-read set of accounts is one of the most important measurement instruments you can have to your company's historic, current and future success or lack of it. It is also a legal requirement in most countries so you will need to make sure you understand exactly what is required and that you feel comfortable you can do it.

Of course there are also benefits to doing your accounts such as the incentive this provides, as well as the opportunity to recoup from the government some of your outgoings (see Chapter 10 for more information).

Do you need an accountant?

If the task of keeping your company's books seems particularly onerous it may well be worth employing the services of an accountant. This is particularly true in the first year of your business, when you will have a thousand and one other things to concentrate on and when you are unlikely to know exactly what records you need to keep and how they should be set out, the format in which the tax return forms need to be completed and how much time you should allow for this etc.

Insight

It may be worth employing the services of an accountant for one year only. This will take the pressure off you in the first year of being your own boss while you find your feet with your new business as well as providing you with a *pro forma* for your accounts (book-keeping and tax return forms) which you can use as a guide in subsequent years.

So what are the benefits of employing an accountant? Certainly doing so will rob you of the unenviable task of having to complete all the necessary taxation forms yourself, to say nothing of having to do the complex calculations, and it will ensure that they are completed in the correct way, are professional looking, and are submitted in a timely fashion. Perhaps the biggest benefit, however, is that a good accountant will very probably be able to save you money. The fact is that tax is a very complicated area and there are so many variations according to the specifics of each individual business that trying to learn them all is a thankless task which you might think is better left to the professionals (unless of course you're going to become your own boss as an accountant!). The only real minus point is the cost, but shop around to find a reputable accountant at a reasonable price (asking other owners of small businesses for recommendations is usually the best method) and it is quite possible that you will find the cost of employing the accountant is less than the tax saving they secure you which of course makes it a no-brainer.

> **'I'm proud to be paying taxes in the United States. The only thing is – I could be just as proud for half the money.'**
>
> Arthur Godfrey

So unless you are very adept at complicated mathematics or have *far* too much time on your hands (in which case couldn't you be putting it to better use elsewhere in your business?) it is almost certainly going to be a good investment employing the services of an accountant, at least for the start of your new business' life.

Case study

'When I first set up my new business I thought very carefully about whether or not to use an accountant. In the end I decided not to. Then after about six months of struggling I realized that I was probably losing more money by having to spend so much time on the book-keeping than it would cost me to employ an accountant!'

Financial housekeeping

When you first become your own boss there are myriad things which require your attention and naturally (and rightly) you want to focus as much of your time and energy as possible on generating work for your business and completing it to the very highest standard to ensure repeat business, so it makes sense to keep your book-keeping as straightforward as possible. Putting in place a sound financial structure for the business is half the battle; the other half is in initiating good financial housekeeping routines – and sticking to them.

SET ASIDE SUFFICIENT FUNDS TO PAY YOUR TAX BILLS

This is something of which a great many people fall foul when they first become their own boss because it is something you never need to consider when you are in paid employ; it simply happens for you, whether you like it or not, without you having to do anything about it. This is because your taxes are collected at source, as you earn them, and so at the end of the tax year you have no outstanding tax liabilities. When you are running your own company however, you will need to pay your annual tax in one lump sum. This is always paid in arrears so provided you set aside, as you go along, that portion of any income generated which represents your tax liability you will automatically have all the money required by the government in taxes at the end of the year already collected, ready and waiting. It really is that simple, but it does require financial discipline; people find themselves in difficulties when they spend or reinvest in the business all the money they are bringing in.

> 'It's not your salary that makes you rich, it's your spending habits.'
>
> Charles A. Jaffe

ENSURE YOUR BUSINESS FUNDS ARE EASILY ACCESSIBLE

Keeping your company's money, or at least a portion of it, in an account which does not require any period of notice in order to withdraw funds is crucial to ensure an uninterrupted cash flow. What happens if your company suddenly faces an unexpected expense? Or if an unforeseen opportunity you would be mad to pass up suddenly arises? What happens if the economy suddenly takes an unexpected turn? By having funds readily available you can circumvent the need to borrow money, either from the bank (which can be very expensive, especially if you find you are not in a position to repay the money as quickly as you had expected), or from the funds you had put aside to pay your tax bill (which can be even more expensive if you find you are not in a position to repay the money as quickly as you had expected).

One word of caution: do not fall into the trap of thinking that you will be able to accurately predict the vagaries of the economy. Even the most experienced finance forecasters can get this badly wrong.

> **'Ask five economists and you'll get five different answers (six if one went to Harvard).'**
>
> Edgar R. Fiedler

KEEP ALL YOUR RECEIPTS SO THAT YOU CAN CLAIM YOUR DUES

As previously discussed you are quite within your rights to offset against your tax burden the taxable portion of any expenses which are incurred solely and wholly for the purposes of your business, and if you are registered for purchase tax you will be able to reclaim that portion of the expenses as well. In addition, you may be able to reclaim from your clients any expenses incurred in the course of your work for them. In all cases, expense claims are necessarily dictated by one thing – receipts, proof of your expenditure. So make sure that you get into the habit of keeping all your receipts, filing them in whatever way makes sense to you (by client, project, chronology etc.) and updating your books accordingly. It is also a good idea to write on each receipt which client you were working for and exactly how the expense was incurred as soon as you are handed the receipt – it can be very difficult remembering the details several weeks (or months!) down the line.

KEEP YOUR COMPANY'S BOOKS UP TO DATE

This is important not only to ensure that facts and figures are fresh in your mind when you fill in your spreadsheets but also to ensure that you do not burden yourself unnecessarily with an onerous task at the end of the tax year – which might be just when you win a large contract which requires all your time. Updating your company's books on a regular basis is also important in ensuring that you always have to hand an accurate and reliable measurement of where your company is versus your forecast.

Insurance

> 'An economist is an expert who will know tomorrow why the things he predicted yesterday didn't happen today.'
>
> Laurence J. Peter

No one can predict the future and despite your best efforts to forecast the incomings and outgoings for your business, it is important to make sure you have adequate insurance in place to cover you and your business in case of emergencies. There are hundreds of companies offering these services with thousands of different products on offer and the range can be quite mind-boggling (as can the price!) so take your time to make sure that you find the right one for your business. Shop around to get the best quote you can for the level of cover you desire based on your company's needs. If your business requires that you have a lot of expensive stock which would need to be replaced should something go wrong, then you will obviously need more comprehensive cover than if you are a consultant or service provider (unless of course any errors in your work could prove costly for your clients, in which case you will need to invest in some heavy duty indemnity insurance). It is also worth considering investing in personal insurance cover to protect you if your income stream unexpectedly dries up, such as a mortgage repayment protector, credit card repayment insurance and insurance against the repayment of personal loans. The majority of policies will not cover you if you find that you are simply not getting any work and thus not receiving any money but most will swing into effect if you are taken ill or suffer an accident, and in some cases they will also pay out if a large confirmed contract falls through (though obviously these policies tend to command a premium).

Funding

'Money talks ... but all mine ever says is good-bye.'
(author unknown)

In the early days of being your own boss there are a great many expenses with which you will have to deal and any extra funds which may be available to you *gratis* would be very welcome. Many people who become their own boss assume that there will not be any funding available to them (why should there be?), but a little research can sometimes prove to be very valuable – you might be pleasantly surprised just what is out there! Local government is often a good starting point but be prepared that even finding out what you may qualify for can be a protracted and tedious process, let alone the application forms and time delays for which you may have to prepare yourself. Do not be easily deterred however as the results may be well worth the effort, particularly in the early stages of your new career. Another good source of information is to ask any friends, colleagues, erstwhile colleagues, friends of colleagues or colleagues of friends – in short, anyone who may know about funding opportunities or may be able to point you in the right direction for further research. Ask about career-specific grants, funding for specialist or general training, access to business loans at preferential rates etc. and initiate the application process at the earliest opportunity – they can take months to complete and even if you are successful you may be kept waiting a good while before you finally receive the funds.

Purchase tax

Most countries levy a purchase tax in one form or another, for example Value Added Tax (VAT) or Sales Tax, and many offer the option of whether or not to register your business for inclusion of such taxes (unless your business generates a turnover in excess of a set annual figure, in which case you will have no option but to add them). Be careful to check the exact requirements placed on your company (in some territories, for instance, it is mandatory to add purchase tax on all sales of certain items) but if you are free to choose whether or not to register your company for the purposes of purchase tax you will need to carefully weigh up the pros and cons. Aside from collecting money for the government (which you may see as either a pro or a con!) there are three main considerations you will need to look at in order to decide whether or not it will be advantageous to you to register your company for purchase tax.

> **Insight**
> Registering your company for purchase tax will not make your offer any more expensive to your clients provided they are also registered for purchase tax.

FINANCIAL ADVANTAGES

As soon as your company is registered for purchase tax you will be entitled to claim back the purchase tax portion of all capital expenses incurred solely for your business. As with any other aspect of company book-keeping, reclaiming the purchase tax portion of expenses is only permitted if the item in question is completely, utterly and solely to be used for your company. So a printer purchased for business correspondence and of which you will have no use for anything in your personal life is accountable for purchase tax purposes, as is the paper, ink etc. it uses. On the other hand, a coffee machine, which will be invaluable in providing you with the necessary stimulus to keep working late into the night but which will also be used for making coffee all the rest of the (non-business) time, or will be used by other members of your family, is not accountable for purchase tax purposes. You will need to decide therefore just how much your company will need to purchase in the way of equipment, IT appliances, tools, etc. which are solely and exclusively for the use of your business, and how much tax you would be able to claim back as a result. Whether there are sufficient financial advantages to be gained to justify the extra workload therefore depends on the nature of your business and whether or not you are likely to be spending sufficient funds on goods liable to purchase tax which are solely for the purposes of your business.

Don't forget that you can only claim back for your business the portion of expenses which are purchase tax.

Example: if the purchase tax rate is 17.5% and you purchase something for £100, the amount you can recoup is not £17.50 but £14.89. This is because the amount before purchase tax would have been £85.11 – it is the purchase tax (£85.11 × 17.5% = £14.89) which brings the total to £100: purchase price (£85.11) plus purchase tax (£14.89) = total cost (£100).

BURDEN – TIME AND RESPONSIBILITY

If you have the option of whether or not to apply for purchase tax registration it is important that you consider the extra burden that doing so would entail and make sure that you are comfortable with it because in most territories the purchase tax returns are due not on an annual basis, as with personal and corporation tax, but more frequently (typically quarterly) and must not be submitted late or you may incur a fine. They must be accurate and presented according to specified requirements (although these are usually set out in a very straightforward manner) and all monies due must be paid at the same time. It should go without saying that purchase tax registration is taken very seriously by governing bodies and you should only go into it if you are willing and able to give it the required attention. You should allow sufficient time every quarter, in addition to that which you have allocated to keeping your accounts up to date, to calculating your purchase tax returns and completing the necessary paperwork, and you must also remember that if you employ an accountant they will need to be made aware of your purchase tax status and may charge an additional fee for the extra work this will give them.

Many territories have introduced provision for companies which do not make in excess of a predetermined annual threshold to apply for admission to a simplified version of purchase tax book-keeping, such as the Flat Rate Scheme (FRS) in the UK. The principle is that instead of having to keep a record of every purchase made and calculate the purchase tax proportion of it to offset against your purchase tax liability (the amount you have collected from your clients on the government's behalf), you keep all the money you receive, including the purchase tax, and simply pass on a percentage of your total earnings, including the purchase tax, instead. The percentage to be deducted varies according to your line of business (if you run a restaurant it will be significantly lower than if you offer a legal service because the quantity of taxable goods you are likely to purchase is far greater) but the calculation remains the same – total turnover including purchase tax multiplied by the specified percentage equals the amount of purchase tax you need to pay. If you opt into such a scheme don't forget that this will be in lieu of reclaiming VAT on expenses so you will not be eligible to claim that as well.

KUDOS

Many people allocate a certain prestige to a company being registered for purchase tax, not least because it can help to give the impression that the company is much larger and has a bigger turnover than is really the case. Whether this perceived kudos is something you think is worth having, or perhaps more to the point whether or not you think it is something your clients will be impressed by, is a consideration you will need to weigh against the extra time and effort it will require and the financial considerations.

KEY THINGS TO REMEMBER

▶ *It is never too early to start getting your new company's finances set up.*

▶ *Make sure you have initiated opening a business bank account well in advance of becoming your own boss – they can take time to set up.*

▶ *Ensure you have sufficient initial capital in place as well as a contingency fund to provide your business with an uninterrupted cash flow.*

▶ *You will need to decide the best trading medium for your business – sole trader or limited company.*

▶ *It is important to keep your company's books updated on a regular basis to ensure accuracy. This will also save you time in the long run.*

▶ *You will need to decide whether or not to employ the services of an accountant.*

▶ *Make sure that you keep receipts for anything you wish to claim back and initiate a filing system for them which makes sense to you and your business.*

▶ *Ensure you keep some funds readily accessible to cope with any unforeseen circumstances.*

▶ *Make sure you have adequate insurance in place to cover you and your business in case of emergencies.*

▶ *Try to find out what funding, if any, might be available to your business such as career-specific grants, funding for specialist or general training, access to business loans at preferential rates etc.*

▶ *Weigh-up the pros and cons of registering your company for purchase tax purposes.*

15

Dealing with clients

In this chapter you will learn:
- *how to recruit for your new business and maintain old contacts*
- *how to foster one-to-one relationships*
- *how to cope with being ignored*
- *how you will balance your workload*
- *how to pinpoint your clients' needs and align your offer*
- *how to fight your corner*

Recruitment

Case study

Q: 'What did you do to ensure you would get work once you left your job?'

A: 'This is the single most important question to address when you are going solo. A good friend once summed it up by asking me if I knew what the first three most important priorities were when setting up as a solo consultant?

The answer: 1. Your first client. 2. Your second client. 3. Your third client.'

Recruitment and retention – securing and retaining clients is fundamental to just about every business in one way or another, and learning the necessary skills is vital to business success, especially if you are your own boss. For many people, the leap to solo working involves becoming their own boss in a similar field to the one in which they have been working, at least initially, so the best method if it is possible is to attract some clients *before* you leave your erstwhile employ. Not only does this ensure your business hits the ground running with established clients eager to employ you from day one, but it also means you take into your new company the goodwill you earned whilst in your old job. After all, it stands to reason – if your clients were not delighted with your work there then they would not be keen to use you again. So taking clients with you is preferable, provided it is morally and legally acceptable. Failing this your best option is to secure new clients through the word-of-mouth recommendations from existing clients (and even if you can take some clients with you into your new business you will probably need to leverage this in order to secure a broader client base as quickly as possible). The third option is to secure new clients through cold approaches, but depending on your line of work this can vary from very challenging to nigh on impossible. Word of mouth means that you are being recommended to someone by someone they already know and, hopefully, whose opinion they respect. If you provide a service, goods etc. which they require then why would they look elsewhere? So, by making your business their easiest and safest option you are halfway to generating work – and income – for your business. So, how do you go about taking clients with you, and how do you generate the best possible return from word-of-mouth recommendations?

TAKING CLIENTS WITH YOU

The first of these is very tricky if you also value retaining a good relationship with your former employer – if not, just get the word out about your new company and ensure you are offering something more, or different, or just plain cheaper than they are. If you do value remaining on good terms with your old paymasters however (and it is almost always preferable to do so), you will need to make sure you are upfront with them about your plans and keep everything transparent so that they feel secure about your actions and do not feel threatened by your intentions. You will then need to establish some common ground to ensure that your new company actually *does them a service* by taking some clients off their hands. Perhaps they are overstretched and can retain their clients' goodwill by outsourcing some work to someone they and their clients know and trust? Or maybe you will specialize in an area which they choose not to cover but which they know is important to their clients and thus they can offer them a more complete service without overstretching themselves, and so on. Crucially, you should make it very clear to them that you are not attempting to muscle in on their territory but rather to support them, and that you will recommend them to any new clients you acquire so the situation will be *quid pro quo*.

WORD OF MOUTH

> **Insight**
>
> Personal recommendations are far, far better than cold advertising – they are easier to implement, cheaper and much more likely to be successful.

How can you influence word-of-mouth recommendations when by their very nature they require other people to do the talking for you? By facilitating the process you can make it as easy as possible for your clients to implement, and by taking pains to ensure the right approach you can make sure they will want to. Firstly, make sure you have a constant supply of promotional materials (business cards, flyers, a constantly up-to-date website etc.) and that you furnish your clients with everything they can pass on to potential future clients. The trick is to make sure that it is something which is genuinely useful to them but which can also be easily passed on and quickly replaced. It stands to reason that if you simply provide a stack of promotional pamphlets or company business cards and ask your contacts to distribute them on your behalf they may well feel somewhat taken advantage of and the chances of them doing as you ask are limited. If, however, you give them a few smart-looking business cards with all your new company's details and which also sport a useful calendar, or perhaps a wall planner, a mouse mat or other useful item replete with the same details and explain to them in a completely honest and upfront way that you would be grateful if they would pass on your details if they feel happy to recommend you, then they are much more likely to assist you. After all, most people accept that this is a necessary part of business life, particularly for a start-up company, and there is every chance that they will respect you and admire your enterprise and be perfectly willing to help. To honour your side of the bargain you need to ensure that if any of your promotional material pays off and one of your clients' contacts does get in touch with you then you respond promptly and helpfully, making your client look good by having recommended someone so obviously capable and efficient. Finally, remember to thank the client who recommended you, thereby further cementing your relationship with them (it might be worth considering offering an incentive in the form of a discount on future work to any clients who so oblige).

Retention

Once you begin to establish a client base you really are already over the most difficult hurdle and with careful management you should be able to continue to build this over time. Just as important, however, is the retention of your clients, vital to business success over the long term.

> '... new-age marketers believe their job is allocating assets in order to achieve desired business results, such as increasing revenue or customer retention.'
>
> Jeff Levitan

Clearly, excellent performance on your part is a prerequisite (why would anyone want to use you again if your work was not to their complete satisfaction?), but just as important is building a relationship. By becoming more than just a passing acquaintance you can help to ensure you stay front of mind for your clients so that you will be their first port of call whenever they need the sort of service you supply – vital if you are competing in a crowded marketplace. It also allows you to stay one step ahead of the competition by keeping in constant contact with your clients so that you will know what they need and when they need it before anyone else does. This affords you the opportunity to be proactive in securing work, excellent both for ensuring a continuous work stream and for looking good to your clients; by being proactive not only do you demonstrate your enthusiasm and proficiency, you also take some pressure off your busy clients by saving them the trouble of coming to look for you. By gently suggesting to them that you are ready and eager to provide them with exactly what they need, and precisely when they need it, at a price with which you know they are comfortable, you really are providing them with excellent service – and all the while gaining work for your company. So your clients get what they desire and at the same time you continue to foster your relationship with them while at the same time ensuring that they do not have the opportunity, or the need, to turn to one of your competitors. This also means that the lines of communication stay open, and it is while you are actively working for a client that you have the single best opportunity to sell in more work.

Fostering one-to-one relationships

A good business relationship between your company and those of your clients is the first step, but just as important is establishing a good client relationship with just one or two specific persons at each company. How often have you heard the phrase, 'It's a people business'? Well the thing is, *every* business is a people business. At each and every company with whom you do business you will be dealing with individuals – so get to know them *as individuals*: what makes them tick, what they need, what they most appreciate in a supplier and what they dislike and so on, to give you the inside track to gaining further work as well as providing them with the very best levels of customer service and cementing an excellent client/supplier relationship. Just as importantly, by keeping in regular contact you may well be able to predict, and circumvent, any possible roadblocks to gaining future work with them.

Insight
Speak when you are not spoken to!

By building a one-to-one relationship and getting to know an individual really well you can often better understand the situation they and their company are in and you will quickly learn to read between the lines. You will be well placed to ask such questions as whether or not this is a good time to be discussing future work with them, and if not why not, and they will feel comfortable in telling you the truth openly and honestly instead of palming you off with excuses and half truths. Do not forget that they may well be embarrassed if their bosses have unexpectedly turned cold on a piece of work about which they had previously seemed keen and they are the messenger left with the uncomfortable job of delivering the news, so it is vitally important that you have established a relationship whereby you can ask those tricky questions which will enable you to ascertain the real reasons why the situation is as it is, rather than just accepting at face value the first reason they give you! By fostering a one-to-one relationship you will be able to dig beneath the surface to discover the real reason (which may not be immediately apparent – is their company experiencing difficulties they do not wish to be made public? Have they taken a strategic decision to move in a different direction? Do they have a cash-flow shortage? Has the department with which you were dealing had their budget cut and they are embarrassed to tell you having previously assured you that they had sufficient budget and this was high priority for them? Are there some internal politics which need to be resolved before they can commission more work?). By keeping close tabs on the situation you can ensure that you are in the best place to capitalize when the optimum moment arises. You will also feel confident that you can discuss the situation with them as it progresses in order to determine your best course of action – perhaps they would appreciate a different sort of service which you provide? Perhaps you just need to give them some breathing space and re-present your offer at a better time, maybe in the new financial year when they have their new budget? Or maybe you can really turn the situation to your advantage and as a result of your close relationship and inside knowledge of their situation and the needs of their business snatch victory from the jaws of defeat by engineering a much larger and more lucrative piece of work in place of the first one.

Being ignored

One of the most frustrating things that every solo worker has to come to terms with when they become their own boss is that sometimes your calls simply will not be returned. When this happens and you begin to feel the pressure of a blank work diary looming, remember not to make yourself unpopular by just becoming a nuisance – after all, you want these people to *want* to work with you. And if a client continuously blanks your calls it is probably because they really have nothing to say to you (yes, it is rude, it would only take half a minute of their lives to return your call and keep you in the picture, but unfortunately that is just the way it is and until they need you more than you need them, that is the way it is likely to stay). The trick is to learn to interpret the signs, and to not be put off too easily and too quickly.

Insight
Don't take 'Yes' for an answer.

If you expect to land every piece of work you chase and for every firm commitment from clients on a project or a piece of work to actually come good you are likely to be very disappointed very often. The hard reality is that a great many things can get in the way of confirmed work actually coming good – clients' priorities may change; your clients may have seemed very excited when you proposed the piece of work but may have grown colder on it since their commitment; your client may still want the work to go ahead but pressures from their bosses may make this impossible etc.

It is worth remembering the old maxim, 'There is no sentiment in business' and a little scepticism about promises of work can go a long way in helping to keep your expectations realistic, to help protect your sensibilities and most importantly to help to ensure that you always have an appropriate amount of work lined up for your business.

Insight

You need to be careful not to overstretch yourself too much, but just about the worst feeling when you have become your own boss is to sit in an empty office at an empty desk staring at a blank screen and knowing you have no work coming in.

Learn to temper each contract won and each promise of future work, however firm, with a little healthy scepticism. Anticipate that every deal will go pear-shaped and be dramatically scaled back or disappear altogether; imagine a worst-case scenario for each project and plan accordingly; grow a skin like a rhinoceros and prepare to be disappointed; importantly, always have a backup plan and know what you will do in the event of a confirmed piece of work falling through. If you can learn to roll with the punches and make the best out of each situation, however bad and unwinnable it seems, and always try to remain optimistic about your business and its future prosperity, then you are halfway to achieving business success; and if you truly believe in your business then this should not be too difficult to do.

Insight

A healthy dose of scepticism can be useful in helping to protect your business from unexpected shortfalls of work, but do not allow yourself to become cynical or your clients may well start to notice and you and your business will quickly become a less appealing proposition to them as a result.

As your business grows, and with it the perceived worth of your work, you may be able to include a compensation clause in contracts so that if a piece of work does fall through you are not left empty-handed but do not count on this, particularly in the early stages of your new business. Take every client's firm commitment in good faith, but remember that no matter how well intentioned it cannot be relied upon, and wherever possible make sure that you get everything in writing; while this certainly does not guarantee that it will come good it can help to focus the client's mind and at least gives you a clear indication of the strength of their commitment at that stage.

'A verbal contract isn't worth the paper it's written on.'

Samuel Goldwyn

LEARN WHEN TO LET GO

No matter how much effort and time you have put into building a relationship with a client and no matter how promising the potential workload with which they could supply you appeared to be, you have to accept that some clients are just a waste of your valuable time, effort and resources, usually not because they mean to be but simply because they do not know how to say 'No'. They may know full well that there is no chance of the work they had promised you materializing and no chance of them being able to give you any other work, but they like you – you have built up a good client/provider relationship and, after all, you are a nice person running a small company – and the sad reality of the situation is that they simply do not want to disappoint you. If and when you know that this is the case it is time to say goodbye, at least for the time being. Remember though, that it is just as important to leave well in this situation as it is to leave your erstwhile employer well and the same principles apply, so make sure that you leave on good terms so that your virtual seat in your client's company will be kept warm should any real work for your company materialize in the future.

Balancing your workload

Two of the biggest challenges facing anyone once they become their own boss are two opposing sides of the same coin: having too much work and not having enough. Both can be detrimental to your business and if not carefully managed they can conspire to cripple it. Getting the balance right is notoriously difficult and it is fair to say that it is something which every soloist struggles with from time to time – or even continually. The feast or famine nature of working for yourself brought about by the need to always have a constant supply of work and the fear of turning any away in case you come to regret it later on and find yourself staring at an empty work diary can be a constant strain resulting in sometimes having to work every single available hour, and sometimes ruing the work deficit.

Case study

'Too much work: Clients love a soloist because they can get much more of your time and energy than they can from a company. Thus they call you up and assume that you are only working for them – they want your energy and fresh positivity on tap 24/7. That's fine when you have two or three projects concurrently, but when it's six or seven it can do your head in. Mix in lots of international travel and you have the recipe for a nightmare: Buenos Aires at 2 a.m., can't sleep but have to be up at 6 a.m. to set up a workshop for client A. Due to an email over supper you are staying up to do a proposal for client B. The phone rings and it's client C wanting a point of view on their project in the next hour and since you answered the phone you can't say no. Meanwhile client D wants a quick chat "in a break" the next day, and clients E, F and G want the agendas for their workshops (weeks away) this week so they can share it with their colleagues.

Too little work: sitting at your desk with nothing to do is a terrible thing for a soloist. There are no internal issues or long-term strategic meetings that you can attend to fill the void of the missing client. It undermines your confidence, your prospects and your bank balance. It is just as bad as having too much on.'

In all probability there are likely to be few occasions in your working life as your own boss when you manage to get the balance just right, but as long as you do not allow the pendulum to swing too far in either direction you should be able to maintain a happy medium to within a tolerable degree.

Pinpointing your clients' needs

Whatever your line of work it is imperative that you pinpoint your clients' needs as accurately as possible ensuring that you have fully understood what they require, including all the parts which are left unsaid! One of the best strategies to employ is to conduct a series of stakeholder interviews so that you can build up a fully rounded picture of your clients' situation and current and future requirements, ensuring that there are no nasty surprises awaiting you further down the line which could have easily been avoided had you understood from the outset the points of view and needs of everyone involved. Conducting stakeholder interviews can often have another beneficial effect – namely affording you the inside track to a company's bosses allowing you to better understand their perceptions of their company's future needs and giving you the time and opportunity to develop a work plan which will help to meet them.

Aligning your offer

It may well be the case that your 'standard' offer is not exactly right for your client's current needs. However, you may be able to modify your offer in order to make it relevant to your client's requirements without sacrificing the integrity of your core offer. This underlines how important it is to ensure you fully understand the needs of your client for any given project rather than simply trying to foist your core offer on them because 'it is what you do'. If your offer cannot be successfully modified then it is better to bow out gracefully and accept that this is one piece of work you will have to pass up on rather than taking it on and achieving limited success with it or worse still, grinding to an embarrassing halt partway through. Remember to make sure however that your client understands the reasons why you will not be working with them on this occasion; they will very likely respect your reasons and the fact that you were open and honest with them, as well as viewing you as a specialist and not a 'Jack of all trades', and this can only be beneficial for your future relationship and your likelihood of securing future work with them.

How to become indispensable

There is a common misconception that simply producing consistently excellent work will be sufficient to cement an excellent working relationship and secure ongoing work. Being excellent at what you do, however, should only be the starting point – indeed, it should be taken as read. In order to become indispensable you need to be able to pre-empt your clients' needs, identify the challenges they will face in their business in the coming months/years and supply them with the answers to their needs before they even know what the questions are, or even that there are any questions! That way you become so much more than simply a service provider – you become an indispensable part of their business machine.

So how can you identify these challenges on your clients' behalf? By fostering the one-to-one relationships we have already looked at and by learning to accurately pinpoint your clients' needs you are already halfway there; the other half is to learn their business inside out and establish a really clear picture of their long-term vision in order to be able to identify as early as possible where on the roadmap you will be able to provide valuable assistance. In this way you will become an extension of your clients' businesses and your clients will quickly begin to perceive you as an indispensable part of their set-up.

Getting paid early

One of the biggest problems many start-up businesses face is managing cash flow and never is this more important than when you are a one person outfit. You may have become your own boss, in charge of the vast majority of the individual elements which make up your business and allow for your business to be successful, but it is an inescapable fact of life that you will remain dependent on other people for some aspects of your business life. Most of these are easily manageable and even if something goes wrong it will not be too much of a difficulty to remedy it, for example, if a supplier is late in providing the materials on which you rely for your business you can turn to an alternative source to furnish you with what you need; it may cost you more to purchase your materials in this way but at least it is an easy and workable solution requiring only the careful navigation of one small obstacle. Not being paid on time, on the other hand, can easily represent a major roadblock to the smooth running of your business and unless you have an alternative source of funding in place it can seriously impact on it. In a worst-case scenario you may be faced with a situation in which several of your clients default on payments at the same time which can be especially crippling – indeed in far too many cases it has proved to be a start-up company's downfall. It is also a fact of life that in the vast majority of cases where this happens the injured party has no recourse to any compensation. It is grossly unfair of course, but the hard reality is that the start-up company simply goes under while their erstwhile clients remain unaffected. Getting paid on time, or preferably early, once you are your own boss therefore is crucially important to any start-up business, particularly if your business model means that you rely on a small number of clients for your business, each paying a substantial amount of money at the end of projects which may be few and far between.

HOW CAN YOU ENSURE PROMPT PAYMENT?

While you will always remain to some degree at the mercy of your clients' efficiency and goodwill, there are some steps you can take to aid this process:

Make sure that all costs, including expenses, are agreed up front, in full and in writing

This means that there will be no nasty surprises on either side when they receive your invoice at the end of a project, which is important not only because it allows you to budget correctly but because nothing slows payment like a discrepancy in the amount on an invoice. Quite simply, until such a discrepancy is ironed out and the value of the invoice agreed, no monies will be paid and it is often the case, particularly with large businesses, that if this situation is allowed to arise you will find yourself dealing not with the client with whom you have established a good working relationship but with someone in the accounts department who does not know you from Adam or Eve. Furthermore, they are unlikely to be appraised of the situation; the type or amount of work which you have completed for their company, what was or was not agreed upfront, why a discrepancy has now come to light and so on. Getting to the root of this is their job and doing so may well prove to be a slow process, particularly as a small supplier like you are unlikely to be their priority. So establishing everything up front and agreeing any necessary changes as you go along is vitally important to getting paid on time. Do not be put off by worrying that you are being over pedantic or making a nuisance of yourself – your clients will almost certainly understand and a transparency in the agreed remuneration is beneficial to both parties.

Agree up front, before you begin any piece of work, the timescale for payment

It may well be that the company for which you are working has an established precedent for the length of time they expect suppliers to wait before payments are authorized (especially true of large multinationals) so make sure you find out what this is as early as you can so that you can budget accordingly. If you feel the timescale to be unfair there may well be room for negotiation, particularly as the sums of money involved are unlikely to prove a major hurdle for any large company, but you will need to get this agreed up front – once the work has been completed, and in some cases as soon as it has begun, it will be too late to make any changes. Remember that however large and faceless the organization may appear you are dealing with a real person, a person who is very likely to understand your situation. This is another instance which proves just how important it is to foster an excellent one-to-one relationship with your primary client, and establishing early on a payment timescale which works both for you and for them will avoid unnecessary headaches further down the line.

Insight

Although most companies try to be fair to their suppliers, some solo workers have experienced situations in which a client's standard payment terms have been as long as six months from the completion of the work (one newly launched business told us they had to wait more than a year for their client to pay up!). This makes accurate budgeting vital (and tricky), especially with regards cash flow – and that is assuming that the client pays on time, and in full.

Insist on a purchase order number

The majority of companies, particularly large organizations, generate purchase order numbers as a matter of course. Smaller companies, however, may not be set up to do this so it will be up to you to instigate it. A purchase order (PO) number is simply a reference code to a particular project or piece of work, a shortcut which can be coupled to details such as the nature and timescale of the work to be undertaken and the agreed remuneration. Therefore, if a company does not normally raise a purchase order code it is a very simple and straightforward matter for them to do so if requested, even on a one-off basis. Having a purchase order reference can prove invaluable if payment is not forthcoming to the agreed timescale as it facilitates your ability to chase the payment and your client's ability to track down your work in their records. Think of it as a shortcut to your work which makes sense to your client's finance department. By having this always to hand and quoted on your invoice you are making their job as easy as possible, and by so doing you are more likely to move to the top of their to-do list and therefore to receive prompt payment.

In the same way it is a good habit to get into to always put your own reference on each invoice to make keeping track of payments easier. It can also be a good idea to quote the appropriate legislation covering late payment to make recovery of interest easier should the invoice not be paid punctually (e.g. 'Late Payment of Commercial Debts (Interest) Act 1998' in the UK). In reality this tends to be extremely difficult to pursue and certainly does little to help foster a good working relationship with a client, but the very fact that the wording is present demonstrates that you are aware of the legislation protecting your business, and this is often enough by itself.

Make sure that you submit your invoice at the earliest opportunity

Find out what is the earliest point at which you can submit your invoice. This is usually as soon as a piece of work has been completed to the client's satisfaction and signed off, but it is always worth checking that this is the case. In some instances it may be acceptable to submit your invoice early to get it into the system so that sign-off signals the end of the accounts procedure, not the beginning. If the company with whom you are dealing knows that yours is a small company they will often make things a little easier for you by accepting earlier invoices, paying in instalments for each tranche of work in a protracted project rather than waiting for it all to be finished etc. Always remember to ask what their payment terms are for small businesses and push to see how flexible these are – you may be pleasantly surprised by what you find.

Once submitted, check to make sure your invoice arrived safely

It is amazing how often emails seem to go astray when they have an invoice attached! Follow yours up with another quick email or phone call to make sure that it arrived safely and that it is with the right person, intact and with the attachment uncorrupted, and that your client's accounts department now have everything they require. Ask your client for a confirmation email to this effect to prevent any confusion at a later date.

Chase your payment *before* it is due

You may feel that you need to wait until the deadline for payment has passed before you begin to chase up your payment – after all, surely it is only courteous to give your clients every opportunity to pay you on time without any hounding from you? And by chasing the payment before it is due are you not risking gaining the unwanted reputation of a worrisome nagger? The simple answer is 'No'. It is perfectly acceptable, particularly for small companies, to chase the progress of payments due to ensure that they are on track to hit the agreed payment date. This will help to ensure that you receive the payment on time, if not a little early, and even in the worst-case scenario where the payment will be delivered late, by chasing it before this occurs you will have made the waiting period as short as possible. You will also have been forewarned about the delay and therefore you will have had the opportunity to forearm yourself by making appropriate short-term alternative funding arrangements. Never be afraid to chase your payment in case it makes you look desperate – it just makes you look efficient and most people will understand that cash flow is a major consideration to any small company.

Foster a one-to-one relationship with someone in the accounts department who will be overseeing payments to your company

Just as we have seen the value of fostering a good one-to-one working relationship with your client, so it can prove invaluable to have a direct line to someone in the accounts or finance department with responsibility for payments. This way, when you need to chase a payment you will know exactly who to go to and, equally importantly, they will know you and therefore be more inclined to ensure that your payment is made promptly.

Thank your clients for prompt payment

If payment is made on time, and particularly if it is made early, be sure to thank your clients for their efforts (both your main client and your contact in the finance department). This way not only will they feel valued and that their efforts have not gone unnoticed but they will also understand just how important prompt payment is to you, ensuring that future payments are more likely to be made on time or even early.

Fighting your corner

One of the most common problems encountered by people when setting up their own business is clients haggling over the cost of your company's services and looking, indeed all too often pressing, for ways to pay you less for the same work. Negotiating a good deal is all part of the process for any client of course, and is absolutely fair play. If the shoe was on the other foot wouldn't you try to secure the best rate you could? Indeed, won't you do just that every time you are dealing with a supplier, securing goods or services for your company? What you need to look out for is when a client tries to push this too far. The most important thing is to ensure you do not get suckered into lowering your day rate. Instead, look at ways to pare down the process you are intending to use so that it takes less time. In this way you are able to still charge the same amount for your time so you have not needlessly reduced your perceived worth while at the same time meeting your client's budget requirements. You have also set a remuneration precedent for the future. Again, try to get everything in writing in order to deter a client from trying to renegotiate the costs after the deal has been agreed.

Case study

'One of the biggest mistakes I made when I first became my own boss was not standing my ground on pricing. In my first year I accepted projects that were below the day rate that I have set myself. I was not confident enough to charge the right amount. Subsequently I have never been able to get back to those clients with my correct day rate and, even more importantly, they did not value my work as highly as my other clients. A bad mistake.'

SHOULD YOU EVER LOWER YOUR PRICES FOR A CLIENT?

The way in which you structure your fees will depend on a great many factors such as what your offer comprises and the type and structure of your business (e.g. information provider, consultancy, service provider) and room for manoeuvre within the pricing structure will vary accordingly from company to company, but one rule remains true across the board: if you believe in your business and genuinely believe that your offer is relevant to the client's current needs and will service them in a targeted and timely manner, that it is truly excellent in its content and delivery and that it is fairly and honestly priced, then there is absolutely no reason why you should lower your price – and the inherent perceived worth of your company's offer.

> ### Insight
> If you do not really believe in your business and your business offer, then it is probably time to go back to the drawing board and rethink your company's proposition and your strategy. After all, if you do not believe in it then why should your clients?

Stick to your guns and point out to the client exactly why the pricing is realistic. Detail the costs to your company, the time effort and expertise required to do the job to the highest standard, and impress upon them that this is just what you will deliver – the very best. Try to make them understand that you are charging a fair and competitive rate for the offer that you provide and at the standard at which you provide it.

Try also to get a really clear idea of what exactly the most important aspects are for your client, bearing in mind that these may well have changed since you took the original brief (if this is the case then it may well be the reason that they do not perceive your offer now to be offering value for money – simply realigning your offer to your client's new needs may be all that is required to remedy the situation). Try also to get a handle on why they are trying to bring down your costs. Is it simply to save them some money to maximize profits (quite possibly) or have their budgets been cut forcing them into the position of needing to find ways to pass on the cost cutting? If so, what is their new budget for your work? Is there scope for flexibility?

In a worst-case scenario you might find yourself forced into the position of having to choose whether to go ahead with the work but at a reduced rate on a strictly one-off basis or whether to pull out altogether. If it does come down to this unenviable decision then you will need to weigh up the situation very carefully. Get it wrong and you could be making a rod for your back, the breaking of which rod might threaten to jeopardize your long-term relationship with your client, or you could be turning away work which you need to ease current cash flow and stemming a potential source of future work. Get it right and you could find yourself getting paid the full amount you asked for, gaining respect for yourself and credibility for your business, or nipping in the bud a client relationship which is destined to sap your time and your energy and ultimately to go nowhere.

KEY THINGS TO REMEMBER

▶ Recruitment of new clients is an ongoing necessity for anyone who becomes their own boss – it is not enough to push hard to recruit new clients only when starting your business.

▶ Equally important is the retention of existing clients which requires you to work hard at building long-term, one-to-one relationships.

▶ Grow a thick skin and never give up on a client – even if they seem to be ignoring you!

▶ Be prepared to realign your offer to match your clients' needs, even mid-project.

▶ By understanding your clients' long-term vision and goals for their business you can make yourself and your company an indispensible part of their business machine.

▶ Getting paid on time, or even early, can be vital to any small business. Do not be afraid to press your clients to make prompt payments.

▶ Always agree costs in full before beginning a project and also establish a timescale for payment.

▶ Always submit your invoice at the earliest opportunity and chase the progress of your payment through the system before it is due.

▶ Try to establish a good one-to-one relationship with someone in the accounts department.

▶ Learn when to let go.

▶ Do not be reluctant to fight your corner over your prices and timescale for payment – just keep track of the market to ensure that they are always fair and competitive.

Conclusion

Taking the leap to becoming your own boss requires a good deal of faith in your own abilities and the courage to leave the safety and comfort of paid employment to take on the risks involved in going solo, but for those who can make a success of it there is little doubt that it is one of the most rewarding ways to make your living, whatever your line of work, and carries with it the deep-rooted satisfaction gained from taking on a significant challenge and seeing it through. Indeed it was interesting to note that of all the people interviewed for this book who have left their jobs to become their own boss, in so many different professions and working in so many different countries, there was not one person who said they regretted their decision, and although their journeys were not always plain sailing, every single one said that they were glad they had taken the opportunity when it presented itself, or that they had engineered it. In fact, many expressed a regret that they had not made the leap to becoming their own boss a lot sooner!

Case study

'Go for it and you'll never look back! But be warned, it changes your life completely and you may never want to work for anyone else ever again!'

So if you think that you have what it takes to leave the confines of paid employment and become your own boss, and if you are as confident as you can be that you have a viable business offer and can make the practicalities of working from home or a new solo or shared office space work for you, your business and your family, then why not seize the moment and take the leap? Just make sure that you are as prepared as you can be for your new working life; then go for it – it may well be the best, as well as the bravest, decision you ever made.

> **'Courage is not the absence of fear, but rather the judgment that something else is more important than fear.'**
>
> Ambrose Redmoon

Appendices

Case studies

In the course of writing this book, people from all around the world and from all business backgrounds who have successfully left their job and taken the leap to becoming their own boss were asked how they had gone about it, what they had found easy or difficult and what they had learned from the process. They were also asked what their top tips would be for anyone else contemplating making the leap. Here are their answers:

Case study 1

This respondent is based in the UK and works in the marketing sector as a consultant and coach.

1 How long have you worked in your current job?

Four years.

2 What were the main factors in deciding to quit your previous employment, or were you made redundant?

Having achieved the goals I had set myself in my old company (to become MD) I began looking around for the next goal. I gradually realized that I did not want any of the jobs the people 'above' me had, they were all political, inward-looking roles. It also dawned on me that now that I was the boss I had no one to look up to and learn from, other than the corporate suits, and I did not want to learn about global business management, P&L reporting or sitting in endless internal meetings discussing company finances. I also looked at my remuneration package and found that despite the fact that I was solely responsible for 30 per cent of the 100-person company's revenues, I was still paid a standard salary and that even with the best bonus the company had ever paid anyone (which they begrudgingly paid me) I was never going to make serious money – the kind of money that the firm's founders had made when they sold the company (and my career) to a big corporate company. All this led me, with much soul-searching (was I being too greedy? was I too selfish? shouldn't I be grateful?), to hand in my resignation. I had to do it several times over six months as it was not accepted and pushed back with offers of more money, a better title (really) and 'we need to think about it', before I finally arranged to meet the top boss for breakfast out of the office with a typed signed letter in my hand. Job done.

3 What were the pros and cons of quitting?

Pros:
  ▷ *Freedom!*
  ▷ *No more coming back having won £1m of new business to find that the company were still £30k off their monthly plan, so we were going to have to stop the chocolate biscuits.*
  ▷ *No more sitting in an 'office'.*
  ▷ *No more urinals.*
  ▷ *No more crap tea.*
  ▷ *No more worrying what 'the parent company' would think of XYZ.*
  ▷ *No more endless calls on my time for no value.*

Cons:
  ▷ *No more guaranteed salary.*

4 Did you consider working for another company? Why did you decide to work for yourself? Did you know you have what it takes to go solo? How prepared did you think you were? How prepared were you in reality (with the benefit of hindsight)?

No. I knew that what I was leaving was a company, with all its financial constraints, mediocrity and pointless internal wrangles. I decided to work for myself because I had seen others go and do it and do it very well. I knew there was a viable business model as a stand-alone consultant. I wanted to focus on the work and just the work. In the end I was very prepared – I spent the last three to four months getting everything ready: stationery, bank account, PC and, crucially, my first client. In reality I was very prepared functionally, but I think I was still unprepared for the actual working at home bit – being in my own home each day with nowhere to go. That was tough to get used to at first. I would sometimes make a big fuss about going up to town with my briefcase etc. only to sit in a Starbucks and do more emails. It was a bit crazy, but it worked for me!

5 What did you do to ensure you would get work once you left?

This is the single most important question to address when you are going solo. A good friend once summed it up by asking me if I knew what the first three most important priorities were when setting up as a solo consultant? The answer: 1. Your first client. 2. Your second client. 3. Your third client. The way it happened was that I left the big corporate on a Thursday afternoon … and I was working for a new client on the Friday. This preparedness paid off in spades in many ways, not just financial. It gave me confidence in my ability and, crucially, it gave my wife confidence that she was not going to lose her home! Also, I had taken the precaution of agreeing to continue to work on one of my old clients, for my previous company, for the first three months. In the end, I did not need this work/income, but I believe it is a very good idea for new 'soloists' just to tide them over for a bit.

6 What were the most daunting/difficult elements of the change to becoming your own boss?

Getting used to working at home. You have to be able not to be endlessly side-tracked by home life or endlessly interrupted by your family who think that, as you are at home, you are fair game to chat to, ask a favour of or 'can you just mind the kids whilst I pop to the shops/have a nap/get my hair cut ...?'

Learning to network better. We all network at big corporate companies – who's who, promotions etc. – but when you are solo it becomes a key skill for survival. It's critical for finding clients as well as suppliers/colleagues to work with, as well as (and for me a really important one) people to chat to and share your daily thoughts with. Suddenly LinkedIn (I never could get on with Facebook or Twitter) becomes a source of reassurance: I am not alone, other people think I'm OK, other people are doing this solo thing too.

7 What are the biggest challenges you face in your working life?

The two biggest challenges I face are similar but poles apart: having too much work, not having enough work.

Too much: Clients love a soloist because they can get much more of your time and energy than they can from a company. Thus they call you up and assume that you are only working for them – they want your energy and fresh positivity on tap 24/7. That's fine when you have two or three projects concurrently, but when it's six or seven it can do your head in. Mix in lots of international travel and you have the recipe for a nightmare: Buenos Aires at 2 a.m., can't sleep but have to be up at 6 a.m. to set up a workshop for client A. Due to an email over supper you are staying up to do a proposal for client B. The phone rings and it's client C wanting a point of view on their project in the next hour, and since you answered the phone you can't say no. Meanwhile client D wants a quick chat 'in a break' the next day, and clients E, F and G want the agendas for their workshops (weeks away) this week so they can share it with their colleagues.

Too little: Sitting at your desk with nothing to do is a terrible thing for a soloist. There are no internal issues or long-term strategic meetings that you can attend to fill the void of the missing client. It undermines your confidence, your prospects and your bank balance. It is just as bad as having too much on.

8 Where do you work? For example, do you have an office in your home? Do you work in the living room/bedroom/garden shed? Do you rent an office space?

I work on the top floor at home. I have turned the spare room into an office. After the first year of being literally in the spare room, perched on the bed and using a dressing table as my desk, I decided to create a real office. It works very well. I have a glass door, nice chairs and a huge desk. It looks and feels like my very own office. Not the product of some cost-conscious corporate 'furnisher' nor a ludicrous glass and metal 'designer' office that looks like a set from some tacky soap opera. It's mine and I feel very comfortable in it.

I am also a member of a club in town. This is a place with somewhere I can go to write or think as well as meet clients one-on-one for a chat, or just a nice place to catch up with old colleagues (who have now gone solo themselves!) over lunch. Money well spent.

9 How do you create your working environment and keep it separate from your living space?

See above. The glass door works a treat.

10 What are the biggest mistakes you've made as a solo worker? What pitfalls would you warn others about?

Not standing my ground on pricing. In my first year I accepted projects that were below the day rate that I have set myself. I was not confident enough to charge the right amount. Subsequently I have never been able to get back to those clients with my correct day rate and, even more importantly, they did not value my work as highly as my other clients. A bad mistake.

11 What have been your biggest successes in terms of working practices? How do you ensure your working life really works for you?

I have a hobby that I take seriously. I like powerboating. I make time in my diary to do it and enjoy every minute of it. This is not a weekend thing – it only takes time from my work diary. It is worth every minute as it energizes me for the client work when I do it. Without this I would get stale pretty quickly.

12 What tips would you give anyone considering quitting their job and going solo?

Check that others have done it before you and survived. Get your own office. Find your first and second clients BEFORE YOU QUIT. Take up powerboating.

13 How do you maximize the flexibility of your working life? For example, do you work from Starbucks twice a week? Do you work only three days a week but for 12.5 hours each day? Do you work only 15 hours per week since this earns you enough to live comfortably and you value having extra free time over extra money? Do you work naked since no one can see you?

Since I went solo, I have never worked over the weekend (other than leaving on Sunday evening for a flight). In big corporate life, I used to work one day every weekend. I take a day out to go powerboating every two weeks (on average). I take eight weeks holiday a year. What I love is that I can choose what balance I want between work and life. If I wanted to I could work half as much and have double the time with my family, but earn half as much. Alternatively I could work as hard as I used to when I was employed and earn loads more. I have found the balance that works for me and I focus on it. It's not a fixed thing – you have to work at the balance every day. But you learn how to flex it as you go along.

I also make sure I get away with my wife, just the two of us, for a weekend once a year. It's very important not to let your work unbalance your home life in a different way by never switching off.

Case study 2

This respondent is based in the UK and works in the financial services sector as a consultant.

1 How long have you worked in your current job?

Six and a half years.

2 What were the main factors in deciding to quit your previous employment, or were you made redundant? What were the pros and cons of quitting?

My role with a large financial services company came to an end, following a merger between two businesses. I was offered the prospect of redeployment but also offered a package, which I took. Most of my best mates had left the company and I felt a sort of fin de siècle *atmosphere. It felt like a great time to move on and do something different.*

3 Did you consider working for another company? Why did you decide to work for yourself? Did you know you have what it takes to go solo? How prepared did you think you were? How prepared were you in reality (with the benefit of hindsight)?

I didn't really consider working for another company. I had had enough of being part of a large corporate undertaking. I was now largely financially secure and wanted two things: first, to do work that I enjoyed; second, the potential of working less in the summer months. I had the advantage of being able to work with a friend and former colleague who had already set up his own consultancy, so I had something of a soft landing. Much later, I started my own company and found it incredibly easy. I wish I had done it sooner. I can't say that I knew everything about what it took to 'go solo', but neither do I think I found myself with too many dilemmas or problems.

4 What did you do to ensure you would get work once you left?

I used my network to establish some contacts with potential sources of work. I don't know whether it was luck, fortunate timing or what, but I secured a large programme of work before I was expecting it or even looking for it. Since then I have built my contacts and most of my work is 'repeat business' in one form or another.

5 What were the most daunting/difficult elements of the change to becoming your own boss?

There weren't too many. I think that my most uncomfortable moment was a piece of work for a huge company that was a former nationalized industry/utility. They were a nightmare – incredibly bureaucratic, inconsiderate and demanding. But the great thing is – I know that now and don't have to work for them again if I choose not to.

6 What are the biggest challenges you face in your working life?

It sounds dreadfully smug, but there aren't any that cause me to lose any sleep! I suppose that if I weren't financially secure, the inconsistency in the volume of work could be a problem. It is rare for the volume to be 'just right'; there tends to be a 'feast or famine' characteristic to the way my work comes in.

7 Where do you work? For example, do you have an office in your home? Do you work in the living room/bedroom/garden shed? Do you rent an office space?

I have an office in my home, which we have recently made much more comfortable and efficient. We should have done that sooner. The nature of my work is that, ultimately I am delivering directly to clients in their premises or in some other venue.

8 How do you create your working environment and keep it separate from your living space?

We didn't do that very well until very recently. I would say that, for most people, it is quite important to do that. Firstly you need to be efficient – not mixing business and domestic material etc. Second, I think most people who work at home need to be able to flick an imaginary switch in their head so that they go into business mode each day. Having a proper office or workshop helps to do that.

9 What are the biggest mistakes you've made as a solo worker? What pitfalls would you warn others about?

Not setting up my own company sooner. I worked as an associate with my friend/former colleague for about four years. It was a complex arrangement that meant I used his company for invoicing and to pay my tax and National Insurance. It began to work to both our disadvantages, so we ended it and I set up my own company.

Not having a PA isn't a problem, but it does mean that I have to do admin., arrange my own travel and accommodation etc. which can be a bit of a pain.

10 What have been your biggest successes in terms of working practices? How do you ensure your working life really works for you?

Just doing what I am good at. It would have been tempting to go flat out for any work and bluff my way through if it wasn't my forte. By finding out what I was good at and sticking to it,

I find my clients trust me and use me again, and I am happy to be doing what I enjoy and am good at. I love it. I try to be well organized and have 'routines' that I follow but, to be honest, I have to work less hard at that than I did when I was in corporate life.

11 What tips would you give anyone considering quitting their job and going solo?

Oh dear, that is a big responsibility. But here goes:
- *Be as sure as you can be that there is a sustainable market for what you plan to do. Don't give up your career or security for something that is transient.*
- *Make sure the numbers add up. Make some pessimistic forecasts about your costs and income and check that you are going to make a reasonable living.*
- *Learn something about accountancy and business finance. You don't have to be an expert, but make sure you understand the basics. Someone I know gets himself into some scrapes, because he is not good with numbers.*
- *Get a reputation for quality and being easy to work with. Customers can cut you off without even an explanation if they want to, so try to deliver! I have encountered some small businesses which are really poor at being customer focused and they suffer as a result.*
- *Understand what causes peaks and troughs in work and plan for it. For example, in my work, it goes deathly quiet in August and around Christmas and New Year, so I make sure that I put money aside to see me through those periods.*

12 How do you maximize the flexibility of your working life? For example, do you work from Starbucks twice a week? Do you work only three days a week but for 12.5 hours each day? Do you work only 15 hours per week since this earns you enough to live comfortably and you value having extra free time over extra money? Do you work naked since no one can see you?

I enjoy the flexibility of being my own boss and working at home. I don't have to work five days a week, so I have time to do other things. You need to plan a little though, to make sure you meet your business obligations. Occasionally, if the sun is shining and there is nothing too pressing, I'll make a spontaneous decision to go to the beach.

I rarely work naked! However it is not unusual to still be in my dressing gown at lunchtime.

I think the greatest buzz is that, occasionally I get to use my friends and family in my work and that is terrific.

Case study 3

This respondent is based in the UK and works in the creative industries and education sector as a consultant.

1 How long have you worked in your current job?

   18 months+.

2 What were the main factors in deciding to quit your previous employment, or were you made redundant? What were the pros and cons of quitting?

   After 18 years working for the same company I was offered a part-time post as opposed to a full-time post due to a complex and poorly handled restructuring scenario involving a colleague on maternity leave. I chose to leave in the end – not much choice really but it was time to go so I took the opportunity. I didn't go quietly as they mismanaged the whole process so badly ... a classic cock-up on their part ... great to watch it unfold. I had to sign a compromise agreement as the managers were on dodgy ground with this 'redundancy'. I made sure I took my pension and haggled a deal.

Pros of quitting: freedom to pursue more creative and imaginative work interests and work in a wider arts based field.

Cons of quitting: being a sole trader and no admin support, plus the loss of a circle of workmates who offered support.

3 Did you consider working for another company? Why did you decide to work for yourself? Did you know you have what it takes to go solo? How prepared did you think you were? How prepared were you in reality (with the benefit of hindsight)?

I was prepared. You must be prepared and think things though. Read up about working for yourself. We had thought it through carefully as a family. We did the figures. I was already set up to work from home. I did not want to work for another company and all the restrictions that would bring. I wanted the freedom to choose when to work and which clients I would work with.

4 What did you do to ensure you would get work once you left?

I took clients with me and a whole host of contacts/networks. I had also set up jobs whilst going through redundancy so I had a seamless transition.

5 What were the most daunting/difficult elements of the change to self-employment?

Going solo. Having to do all the admin tasks and typing myself. Doing the books. Setting up tax and accountancy support. Sorting out the official stuff and getting it right from the start. Setting up systems/bank accounts, IT kit. Getting the right level of insurances.

6 What are the biggest challenges you face in your working life?

Making sure I have enough work in the diary; dealing with BT; keeping healthy so I can work. Keeping cheerful. Knowing how and when to nag clients when they don't pay up.

7 Where do you work? For example, do you have an office in your home, do you work in the living room/bedroom/garden shed? Do you rent an office space?

I work in a room in the house dedicated as an office space. I had done this for my previous job so I am used to it. It is off the kitchen which works well. The family keep out unless they need to nick paper or scissors! My laptop is out of bounds to anyone but me. It is important that these boundaries are set up from the start.

8 How do you create your working environment and keep it separate from your living space?

The room is mine and I set it up and run it as an office with a separate phone line and number different from the family phone line. I also have my own broadband set up ... this keeps all the bills separate. No one else uses my room or my kit.

9 What are the biggest mistakes you've made as a solo worker? What pitfalls would you warn others about?

Pitfalls: taking on too much work for fear of getting none; not putting holidays into the work schedule until it's too late. Knowing when to stop and switch off the laptop. Working at weekends – avoid it. Make time for work and time for play. Not doing a proper business plan at first – I have now and it's a great tool for seeing how far you have come since the start.

10 What have been your biggest successes in terms of working practices? How do you ensure your working life really works for you?

Early days but successes so far: breaking out of schools focused work and into longer arts-focused projects with arts organizations. Running a big arts project successfully.

Going for jobs I would never have thought possible. Completing an MA whilst setting up a business ... not recommended! Keeping up networks and contacts. Developing my IT skills and money management.

11 What tips would you give anyone considering quitting their job and going solo?

Get a good accountant. Make friends with a local printing firm for headed paper. Set aside correct funds to pay your tax bills. Keep it in an account that gives interest but you can access easily. Keep receipts so you can claim. Get a good IT support worker when things go wrong. Make time for holidays, the gym and family. Go on the free Business Link courses – you get some good tips. NatWest business section were helpful when I first began. Talk to colleagues. Make time to network. Get a good website and learn to promote yourself. I had envelopes printed with my logo on the front which always cause a comment!

12 How do you maximize the flexibility of your working life? For example, do you work from Starbucks twice a week? Do you work only three days a week but for 12.5 hours each day? Do you work only 15 hours per week since this earns you enough to live comfortably and you value having extra free time over extra money? Do you work naked since no one can see you?

I love phoning up head teachers or senior managers from home whilst I am in my pyjamas. I love going on holiday when schools are mid-term. It's great to go shopping and have lunch when everyone else is working. I make one day a week a 'me day' so I can recharge my batteries, go to the gym, meet friends socially, catch up on day time TV etc. I am earning the same working four days a week as I was when I was full time. My health has improved. I am nicer to live with and I am more creative than I have ever been.

Case study 4

This respondent is based in the UK and works in the marketing sector as a research specialist.

1 *How long have you worked in your current job?*

Four years.

2 What were the main factors in deciding to quit your previous employment, or were you made redundant? What were the pros and cons of quitting?

I took voluntary redundancy when I heard a round of redundancies were looming. I wanted to have more freedom and flexibility, as I had two young children, and decided working for myself would be worth trying so as to achieve a better work/life balance.

3 Did you consider working for another company? Why did you decide to work for yourself? Did you know you have what it takes to go solo? How prepared did you think you were? How prepared were you in reality (with the benefit of hindsight)?

I didn't consider working for another company. I decided to work for myself so as to be master of my own time and better manage my workload etc. I wasn't remotely prepared and I knew I wasn't. I was fortunate enough to know that my salary wasn't completely essential for our survival.

4 What did you do to ensure you would get work once you left?

Spread the word that I was freelancing.

Came up with a name and an identity for my company to give it credibility – branding.

5 What were the most daunting/difficult elements of the change to self-employment?

Punching above my weight with clients initially. Having to stand entirely on my own two feet with no backup.

Lack of admin help and needing to get to grips with how to do accounts etc.

6 What are the biggest challenges you face in your working life?

Time management – not working all hours that God sends – having the confidence to believe in the work I have done without constantly feeling a need to improve it.

7 Where do you work? For example, do you have an office in your home? Do you work in the living room/bedroom/garden shed? Do you rent an office space etc.?

Office upstairs at home. The fact that it is upstairs, and away from the main living space is critical!

8 How do you create your working environment and keep it separate from your living space?

By having it physically away from the living space.

By giving it a more 'officey' look and feel.

9 What are the biggest mistakes you've made as a solo worker? What pitfalls would you warn others about?

Taking on too much.

10 What have been your biggest successes in terms of working practices? How do you ensure your working life really works for you?

> ▷ *Setting up a brand and identity – giving credibility to my work and allowing me to charge more!*
> ▷ *Hiring a proper accountant to do it all for me.*
> ▷ *Sub-contracting to ease the workload but ensuring I work with the other person – i.e. not handing over projects, but sharing the workload and being very careful who I employ.*
> ▷ *Putting a mark-up on the costs of those I employ – creaming cash off the top and doing less work myself!!*

11 What tips would you give anyone considering quitting their job and going solo?

> ▷ *Go for it and you'll never look back! But be warned, it changes your life completely and you may never want to work for anyone else ever again!*
> ▷ *Beware of getting too used to the freedoms of being alone in an office – fart when you want to, pick your nose etc. – you then have to be REALLY careful not to let this happen when with other people!*
> ▷ *Always get dressed in the morning!*
> ▷ *Make a clear line between home life and work life by working in a different space in the house – not the living room and NEVER the bedroom.*

12 How do you maximize the flexibility of your working life? For example, do you work from Starbucks twice a week? Do you work only three days a week but for 12.5 hours each day? Do you work only 15 hours per week since this earns you enough to live comfortably and you value having extra free time over extra money? Do you work naked since no one can see you?

> ▷ *Go to the gym twice a week between 9 and 11.*
> ▷ *Stop work at 3 p.m. one day a week to look after the kids.*

> ▷ *Take time off to take kids to appointments within hours,*
>   *watch school plays etc.*
> ▷ *Very clear boundaries and strong self-discipline – never*
>   *work in the evening unless pre-arranged on a project*
>   *(e.g. when moderating a focus group).*

Case study 5

This respondent is based in the UK and works in the defence sector
as a Programme Manager.

1 How long have you worked in your current job?

Two years.

2 What were the main factors in deciding to quit your previous
employment, or were you made redundant? What were the
pros and cons of quitting?

I chose to leave my previous employer. Main factors:
> ▷ *I had achieved my main goals with them.*
> ▷ *I had reached the age when the pension was payable*
>   *(i.e. outside of the pension trap).*
> ▷ *I had gained training, a range of sought-after skills,*
>   *qualifications and experience that made me marketable*
>   *and attractive as a consultant.*

Pros of quitting:
> ▷ *The potential to transfer skills to another sector.*
> ▷ *New challenges.*
> ▷ *The opportunity to draw on a pension at the age of 39.*
> ▷ *Greater potential future rewards.*
> ▷ *The chance to run my own business.*
> ▷ *More choice regarding shaping my future career path.*
> ▷ *No glass ceilings.*

▷ *Choice of whether to take six-month deployments (secondments) rather than being posted to such as appointment.*

Cons of quitting:
▷ *Leaving a very secure, reasonably well paid career for a much more uncertain existence.*
▷ *Greater potential risk (but also greater potential rewards).*
▷ *Turning my back on a managed career path without the prospects of further promotion.*

3 Did you consider working for another company?

I considered further employment but all the psychometric tests pointed me towards the need to work for myself and exploit entrepreneurial aspects of my character.

4 Why did you decide to work for yourself?

An opportunity allowed me to become a consultant within a familiar area ... this would allow me to set up the business, run it and look for other areas of business to expand into. This approach enabled an easy transition to consultancy, limited the risk and demanded minimal capital expenditure to set up the company.

5 Did you know you have what it takes to go solo?

I had reasonable confidence in my own abilities but had not previously run my own business so there was always going to be some learning to do.

6 How prepared did you think you were? How prepared were you in reality (with the benefit of hindsight)?

I found it easier than expected. There were a lot of people within my network who provided some outstanding advice and assistance.

7 What did you do to ensure you would get work once you left?

I was lucky because the Royal Navy have a very good and comprehensive resettlement package. This provides some general resettlement courses but I focused some weeks of training on 'Small Business' and 'Managing Successful Businesses' courses. These ensured I started my business correctly and eased my way into profit.

8 What were the most daunting/difficult elements of the change to self-employment?

Nothing was too daunting. I quickly gained contracts so was able to work and gain turnover for the company. Doing the books, setting up VAT/PAYE/NIC etc. was new but I gained advice from friends and my accountant and these are really quite simple once set up.

9 What are the biggest challenges you face in your working life?

As a contractor with a key customer, there is vulnerability over what the future will hold. Whilst it would be ideal to have several customers, to date this has been difficult because my current contracting outputs require near full-time effort … the main challenge is therefore to try and retain breadth/ experience in order to compete for new work (whilst still doing a full-time contract). With the requirement for my skills currently outstripping my company's capacity the key question is whether I should employ other consultants and expand.

10 Where do you work? For example, do you have an office in your home? Do you work in the living room/bedroom/garden shed? Do you rent an office space?

I have an office at the company but due to the nature of much of my work I spend most of the time at the client's premises.

11 How do you create your working environment and keep it separate from your living space?

I am either separated at the client's premises or I am at my office at work.

12 What are the biggest mistakes you've made as a solo worker? What pitfalls would you warn others about?

I have been very lucky in that I have not come across any significant issues yet (I have had no break in contracting periods; remuneration is great; I just wish I had more time to think about the future direction for the company!). The only regret I have is that I wish I had done it earlier ... but this was not realistic given I needed the qualifications and experience, and I was in a pension trap.

13 How do you ensure your working life really works for you?

This is probably a weak area because I am now working extremely long hours and of course this is how you gain turnover. It is however important to get the right work/life balance and whilst we accept that work will be and will remain demanding we have ensured that reasonable breaks are taken each year.

14 What tips would you give anyone considering quitting their job and going solo?

Understand and analyse the reasons for doing it. If you are convinced that you have the idea/character and you can succeed without taking unreasonable risks then develop a strategy and test your business plan against your work and personal life goals ... but note that you need to be 150 per cent committed and determined to succeed from the start... complacency is not an option.

15 How do you maximize the flexibility of your working life? For example, do you work from Starbucks twice a week?

Do you work only three days a week but for 12.5 hours each day? Do you work only 15 hours per week since this earns you enough to live comfortably and you value having extra free time over extra money? Do you work naked since no one can see you?

With five children to feed and support I could only just exist if I was to work two to three days a week. I therefore try to work five days a week but there are many times when I will have to work more!

Case study 6

This respondent is based in New Zealand and works as a consultant and coach.

1 How long have you worked in your current job?

I'm not sure I'd call it a job – it's more of a vocation. Technically the company has been going for one year, but my business partner and I have been doing this informally for five years.

2 What were the main factors in deciding to quit your previous employment, or were you made redundant? What were the pros and cons of quitting?

If you read the Millionaire Mind *[by Thomas J. Stanley], it talks about most millionaires never fitting anywhere. I don't fit anywhere – I don't even fit with misfits. My family are 'done well working class' and I went to an English public school – which gives me feet in both areas. I am naturally curious and eccentric, friendly but fundamentally I have always felt I look at things from the outside. For many years I struggled to find a home – I finally realized the only true home is the culture you create. I guess that was the driving force behind our decision to emigrate – and my decision to leave the directorship I held here. I have always wanted to forge new territory, to create things that haven't been made before.*

Pros of quitting:
  ▷ *Self-empowerment.*
  ▷ *Challenge.*
  ▷ *Huge personal growth on all levels – personal, spiritual and emotional.*

Cons of quitting:
  ▷ *It's cold outside – it is very lonely starting things up.*
  ▷ *People in corporates get rose tinted about the sense of freedom. You don't get to enjoy this for years, it's just bloody hard work.*

3 Did you consider working for another company? Why did you decide to work for yourself? Did you know you have what it takes to go solo? How prepared did you think you were? How prepared were you in reality (with the benefit of hindsight)?

No, I didn't consider working somewhere else. No one is ever prepared to work solo except God – I am quite serious, 'experience is something you gain when you no longer need it …'. You have to be prepared to embrace the fact that you've got a vision and you don't know what you don't know – you have to learn to dance in uncertainty.

4 What did you do to ensure you would get work once you left?

At first I was doing consulting for marketing – I ensured I had two clients who would come with me when I left. Whatever you do – cushion your journey into self-employment by either a) trialing your product while you have a day job or b) getting clients in advance of leaving.

5 What were the most daunting/difficult elements of the change to self-employment?

I call it the cup-of-tea syndrome. There is no one to make you a cup of tea and that applies to everything. So you have to get focused on a) what you are good at and b) what you aren't, and ensure you get help with the latter – most small businesses are small minded and try to save money by trying to do everything. Focus on where you can generate revenue fastest and don't waste time on anything else.

6 What are the biggest challenges you face in your working life?

There are so many – the lead one was spending half of our wealth on a dream and one sentence killed it, having invested two years of time and energy making it happen. Watching a dream die is hard – it hits you in every possible way – and you know, I'd still make the same choices again because they brought me new dreams, but at the time I was gutted – I felt like I had been bereaved.

7 Where do you work? For example, do you have an office in your home? Do you work in the living room/bedroom/garden shed? Do you rent an office space?

I am peripatetic – I chose the environment which I think will best allow me to complete a task.

8 How do you create your working environment and keep it separate from your living space?

I have a separate study and a lightbox I turn on to indicate I'm working – it stops me half doing things.

9 What are the biggest mistakes you've made as a solo worker? What pitfalls would you warn others about?

You can read about this again and again ... but it is experience that allows you to 'get it'. Focus on who you want to be in your working life not what you want to do – get very clear about who you are as a person. Ask yourself this – okay, from tomorrow I have no income at all, no fixed income, and I have

to make it myself. If that fills you with excitement and fear –
move towards being a solo worker. If all you feel is castrated
by fear – celebrate the role and career you are in and become
the best you can be at it ... Be motivated by a positive future,
not a sense of 'life must be better than this'.

10 What have been your biggest successes in terms of working
practices? How do you ensure your working life really works
for you?

Look after yourself: meditate, exercise and inspire yourself daily.

11 What tips would you give anyone considering quitting their
job and going solo

Go to 9.

12 How do you maximize the flexibility of your working life?
For example, do you work from Starbucks twice a week? Do you
work only three days a week but for 12.5 hours each day? Do
you work only 15 hours per week since this earns you enough to
live comfortably and you value having extra free time over extra
money? Do you work naked since no one can see you?

I used to be very rigid about appointments and driving
things forward. I find it best now to leave a lot of time open
to pursue goals – organic structure allows for, in my case,
a more effective pursuit of order than either being organic
(say a Branson) or structured alone.

You need to find your personal style.

Case study 7

This respondent is based in the UK and works in the theatre and
entertainment sector as a manager and producer.

1 How long have you worked in your current job?

Since June 2007.

2 What were the main factors in deciding to quit your previous employment, or were you made redundant? What were the pros and cons of quitting?

I acquired full industry knowledge as head of touring for a major theatre producer. After five years there, I felt it was the time to seek a different challenge and was offered a role as a producer/creative for a television company. This was offered on a freelance basis initially, which opened the door for me to start up my own theatre company to run alongside the television work. There was no conflict of interest, so that was fine, and I had been asked time and time again during my years in my former job whether I would consider booking/ managing theatre tours away from their shows. I wouldn't and couldn't do so then, now I could. It also meant that ten years of theatre would not go to waste.

3 Did you consider working for another company? Why did you decide to work for yourself? Did you know you have what it takes to go solo? How prepared did you think you were? How prepared were you in reality (with the benefit of hindsight)?

Yes indeed, clearly with one hat I was indeed working for another company – albeit from a self-employed platform. However, for the theatre company, it did require some bravery and no, I certainly did not know I had what it takes and indeed whether I still have! I was opportunistic frankly, I knew I had the safety margin of the television work and pay, so I could sensibly afford to take the risk with my own venture. This to me made most sense – a calculated risk. Many people jump in too soon, and without requisite experience. Some are brilliant and work out a way to thrive, but I have seen many more fall by the wayside in theatre. My strategy was clear – a balanced risk, ten years of contacts and a sensible, small-starting business plan. The only thing I needed to do was work all hours, I don't mind that.

4 What did you do to ensure you would get work once you left?

I secured a great big sexy contract! Basically, through a strong friend and contact, I was offered the opportunity to tour product for the Menier Chocolate Factory. They are basically the hottest property in theatre at the moment – started in 2005, and in that short time, they have transferred many of their productions to the West End and a couple to Broadway. They have racked up many Olivier Awards and last year broke the all-time record for a debut Broadway producer with the number of Tony nominations received for Sunday in the Park with George. *I would be touring their West End hit* Little Shop of Horrors *and I simply thought, 'How can I fail?' For me, the main skill was being the one to be approached, and that's where ten years of being at the top of my profession paid off. If you're good at what you do, people will approach you …*

5 What were the most daunting/difficult elements of the change to self-employment?

The accounting. Can't stand it, or understand it. Thank God for my Dad – he had just retired and offered (actually demanded) to take on my books. Just as well, he knows I would muck it all up, forget to pay my National Insurance or whatever.

6 What are the biggest challenges you face in your working life?

The utter constancy of proving yourself. Quite rightly, you're only as good as your current results, so you must always strive to keep working hard, networking, delivering … Theatre is in the doldrums at the minute, a victim of the credit crunch, and it has impacted on the risks being taken in our industry. I am a go-between between theatres and producers and somehow

I must persuade both sides to keep investing in each other.
It isn't easy …

7 Where do you work? For example, do you have an office in your home? Do you work in the living room/bedroom/garden shed? Do you rent an office space?

Home office. Not the Home Office, just to clarify!

8 How do you create your working environment and keep it separate from your living space?

It is a separate room, with office-type stuff in it (computer, fax/scanner/printer, pointless rubber plant, empty files etc). Very seriously though, I think that is vital, you need to have a room which does not feel too homely, otherwise you'll be prone to slips of discipline. Never, ever work in earshot of a television!

9 What are the biggest mistakes you've made as a solo worker? What pitfalls would you warn others about?

I've been quite cautious so far, so I don't think I've made any howlers. As I said before, I've seen many people fail, and the most common cause is that they over-reach, get too excited when the good things happen, and over-invest (or even over-celebrate).

10 What have been your biggest successes in terms of working practices? How do you ensure your working life really works for you?

I left the film company after a year as it was failing badly. Being my own boss though means I was able to set up my own film company to achieve the things I wanted from that industry too. I would say that my biggest success has simply been my ability to work damn hard and do the sensible things (can't stress enough the importance of networking when you work for yourself – be friendly and supportive to everyone else in your industry and you have a chance that they will be the same back!).

I guess to answer the second part, it all patently works for me because I adore theatre and film, I love the people and the excitement of it all. It is seriously addictive. I don't, frankly, find the hard work of it all to be particularly hard work. Top tip then, and it's damn obvious, before you work for yourself, make sure you love the work. You'll have no one to fall back on if you feel de-motivated ...

11 What tips would you give anyone considering quitting their job and going solo?

Think long and hard before you make the leap. Research all the boring stuff, the legal requirements, the accounting, the VAT thresholds etc. Then get some guarantees of work in before you make the leap, don't start cold. Then be rigid and sensible with your business plan. Don't over-stretch, and don't get drunk after the first deal. And finally, and I would think this stands up for most industries, have a little budget for networking/entertaining and go and use it! You get work by meeting people, not by sitting at home hoping they'll call you. You need to hustle, laziness is stupefying if you are thinking you can generate your own living.

12 How do you maximize the flexibility of your working life? For example, do you work from Starbucks twice a week? Do you work only three days a week but for 12.5 hours each day? Do you work only 15 hours per week since this earns you enough to live comfortably and you value having extra free time over extra money? Do you work naked since no one can see you?

I manage a few jobs on the side, but there again, I'm in an industry where you can do that. I can see one person in media for a drink and cut three deals with him/her depending upon which company hat I wear at any one point. I would say the key for me is to be flexible. Someone once taught me that I could do all this for myself if I was hungry and had a phone line. They were right. Hunger is motivation – the get-up-and-go within. The phone line is merely the vehicle to make things happen from hour to hour. If I find I have spent two days indoors trying to make business happen and it hasn't, you can bet your last penny that I won't be spending a third day indoors. I'll be out hustling …

Case study 8

This respondent is based in the US and works in the marketing sector as a qualitative researcher.

1 How long have you worked in your current job?

11 years since I have gone solo; 18 years as a Qualitative Researcher.

2 What were the main factors in deciding to quit your previous employment, or were you made redundant? What were the pros and cons of quitting?

I wanted a change in life. I therefore decided to move country (moved from the UK to Italy and then from Italy to the US). I wanted to explore new possibilities and take on new challenges. I quit my job – I needed something new and exciting.

Pros of quitting:
  ▷ *The feeling that everything is possible and it is up to you: total freedom!*
  ▷ *Nobody to rely on, nobody else to blame … or to be accountable to.*

Cons of quitting:

> ▷ *Fear of the unknown, of leaving something known and comfortable.*
> ▷ *You are faced with a white canvas and it is up to you (and destiny) to paint the picture.*

3 Did you consider working for another company? Why did you decide to work for yourself? Did you know you have what it takes to go solo? How prepared did you think you were? How prepared were you in reality (with the benefit of hindsight)?

At the time I considered working for another company, I think that a part of me wanted a sense of security and a feeling of belonging to something bigger. After interviewing with a few companies nothing seemed right. Immediately after quitting I had a few projects commissioned, thus the transition was quite easy and smooth ... natural. I grew up thinking that it was all about climbing the corporate ladder ... circumstances changed my framework, my paradigm ...

4 What did you do to ensure you would get work once you left?

Networked, contacted old colleagues, old friends. The transition from corporate life in the UK to Italy was easy. The most challenging aspect for me was moving to the US, since I had absolutely no business contacts in this country ... but tapping into my European network I was able to develop a client base in the US. The challenging nature of the situation unveiled aspects of myself I was not aware of.

5 What were the most daunting/difficult elements of the change to self-employment?

Having to deal with the small things ... from finding the right accountant, to fixing IT issues, from buying the right PC to finding support. I was used to focusing on my work and on my clients' needs ... all of a sudden I had to deal with practical matters ... I am not very good at that! The most challenging

was finding the right help and support ... I made a few
mistakes.

6 What are the biggest challenges you face in your working life?

The biggest challenge is not being able to plan long term.
There are times when I am swamped with work and work
around the clock. Other times work can be slower and I
have quite a bit of free time. The work flow can be very
unpredictable, I hate turning work down ... just in case the
next month is not as busy. This makes it difficult to plan
vacations with the family or time off. I have become better at it.

7 Where do you work? For example, do you have an office in
your home? Do you work in the living room/bedroom/garden
shed? Do you rent an office space?

I have a separate office building on my property – it is a large
open space where I have all my stuff and I feel I have the
space to think and move around.

8 How do you create your working environment and keep it
separate from your living space?

Having a separate office really helps – I shut my office door
and I am in my own working world. It is MY WORKING
ENVIRONMENT – to inspire and stimulate. I play music,
have plants, have a kitchen area ... if I need to I can go
there at 4 a.m. and make my calls to Europe and nobody
notices ... the kids wake up at 7 a.m. and I can be 'back
home' for them ...

9 What are the biggest mistakes you've made as a solo worker?
What pitfalls would you warn others about?

My main mistakes revolve around the type of people I chose to
help me. I chose the wrong accountant just because I was in a
rush to find somebody. I am still trying to sort her mess out.

I also kept clients that were not that profitable out of fear and concern of not having enough work, preventing me from focusing on the more profitable clients who gave me the more interesting and challenging projects. By saying yes to everybody the first couple of years I worked all the time – my family ended up being neglected. I think I have finally found the right balance, but it took a while.

10 What have been your biggest successes in terms of working practices? How do you ensure your working life really works for you?

My biggest success is the fact that I can run a profitable business, much more profitable than what I was making while working for a corporation and still have time to spend with my family, live where I want (in a remote area surrounded by wilderness), travel all over the US and the world and pursue my personal interests. I have learned that there is time for work and personal time and the two are separate. I love my work but I have to draw a line in order to be able to give time and energy to my family.

11 What tips would you give anyone considering quitting their job and going solo?

The first thing would be to do some self-analysis and assess if they are truly the independent types. I have met many people who thrive in an organization and if they do, this is probably not for them. You have to be fiercely independent, then you will love going solo … anything else is a compromise.

From a practical point of view it is important to make sure they have business lined up for the first six months to a year. Ask colleagues who have done it before concerning the pros and cons in their specific industry. Make sure you have enough savings set aside in case things don't go as planned at the beginning. Have a clear vision of the six-month, one-year *and five-year plans. Have a backup plan in case things don't go as envisioned. Be proactive in meeting people in the same industry to keep up with trends. Avoid isolation.*

12 How do you maximize the flexibility of your working life? For example, do you work from Starbucks twice a week? Do you work only three days a week but for 12.5 hours each day? Do you work only 15 hours per week since this earns you enough to live comfortably and you value having extra free time over extra money? Do you work naked since no one can see you?

Flexibility is what enables me to think ... It is a sine qua non ... it is not about maximizing it. If you go solo your motto is: 'I am flexible ... ergo sum.' I felt stifled in the corporate world – I lacked breathing space. Flexibility does not mean that I work less ... I work more. I am a bit of a workaholic, I could work all day and all night, in my pyjamas, clothes or whatever ... I get a sense of excitement from my work. However, there are other things that are more important such as my family, friends, life experiences ... I therefore try to balance things out. I may spend a month focused on my projects and the next month I spend more time with the people I care for, doing things like exploring with the kids, spending time with them doing what they enjoy. There is no rule, I am flexible and I have to be flexible. One thing I have learned is to relinquish some control and have people work for me to do some of the time-consuming things I don't enjoy. This has freed up a lot of my time.

One last thing ... it helps that my husband is the stay-at-home person ... he represents stability for my kids and for me. I can be flexible because somebody else is there for me, since the world around is not that flexible.

Chapter quizzes

Test your knowledge of some of the key elements of becoming your own boss by using these quick quizzes to determine in which areas you are lacking or to revise what you have learned. Each quiz focuses on one chapter of the book for easy reference should you wish to build your knowledge in this area.

Chapter 1 quiz

WEIGHING THE OPTIONS

Why do you want to become your own boss? Do you fully understand the implications, including the downsides? Use this quiz to help you determine the options available to you, and your best course of action.

1 *Why do 95 per cent of all new businesses fail?*
2 *What are the key motivating factors driving you to quit your job and become your own boss?*
3 *What do you predict will be the biggest drawbacks to becoming your own boss?*
4 *What do you predict will be the biggest benefits to becoming your own boss?*
5 *What changes do you think you will need to make to your current lifestyle in order to facilitate a smooth transition to becoming your own boss?*
6 *What are the downsides to leaving paid employment, and what are the downsides to becoming your own boss?*
7 *What are the upsides to leaving paid employment, and what are the upsides to becoming your own boss?*
8 *Are there elements of your current job you could change to give you what you need in your working life?*

9 *Why might life coaching prove beneficial for you?*

10 *How much is your desire to become your own boss influenced by other people? How certain are you in your heart of hearts that the move is right for you?*

Chapter 2 quiz

ARE YOU CUT OUT TO BE YOUR OWN BOSS?

Do you have what it takes to make it as your own boss? Use this quiz to make sure you understand the requirements of running your own business and your particular strengths and weaknesses.

1 *Do you feel you are a natural candidate for becoming your own boss? How likely do you think you are to succeed?*

2 *In what ways do you hope/expect the move to becoming your own boss will change you as a person?*

3 *What changes do you think you will need to make to your current lifestyle in order to facilitate a smooth transition to becoming your own boss?*

4 *What support do you think you will need and from whom?*

5 *Are there any additions to your skill set which will be required?*

6 *What are your greatest work-related strengths and weaknesses?*

7 *What is a psychometric profiling test and why is it important to anyone considering becoming their own boss?*

8 *What are your key personality traits?*

9 *What are your key work-related aptitudes and attitudes? How well do these translate to becoming your own boss?*

10 *Is becoming your own boss really your best option? How fully have you explored changing your role with your present employer or doing the same sort of job but in a different company?*

Chapter 3 quiz

STAYING PUT

Is staying in your current job but improving your situation your best option? Use this quiz to help you determine the possibilities open to you should you decide to remain where you are.

1 *Why might not becoming your own boss be the bravest and best decision you have ever made?*
2 *What changes do you need to implement in your work life in order to achieve the career you really want?*
3 *Where do your business and personal priorities lie?*
4 *If you could only change three things in your work life what would they be?*
5 *Over what timescale is it realistic to expect the changes to take place?*
6 *How will you monitor the changes and review their progress?*
7 *What would you most like to improve about your position within the company – job description, salary, holiday entitlement, title etc.*
8 *Would working from home part time help you to achieve a better work life?*
9 *Would your company be amenable to you working from home part time? How can they help you to implement the changes?*
10 *What would be your ideal working week? How many hours would you work each day and over how many days would the hours be spread?*

Chapter 4 quiz

QUITTING YOUR JOB

Are you certain that quitting your job is your best option? Do you have a plan of how to execute your leaving to maximum advantage? Use this quiz to ensure you have covered all the bases for leaving well.

1 *Have you reached the end of the road in your current job? Do you really want to stay where you are for the foreseeable future?*
2 *Have you seen other people in your industry successfully make the move to becoming their own boss? Is there any reason why you cannot emulate, or better, their success?*
3 *Once you have made up your mind to leave your job what should your first conversation with your employer be about?*
4 *What can you learn from your bosses which will help you to refine your offer once you have gone solo?*
5 *When is the best time to quit your job?*
6 *What steps can you take to ensure you leave your old job to maximum advantage?*
7 *What sort of database should you compile? And when and where?*
8 *Why do you need the services of an employment lawyer?*
9 *What practical elements of your new business can be set up before you quit your job?*
10 *What points of convergence between your old and new careers can you capitalize on?*

Chapter 5 quiz

WHAT BECOMING YOUR OWN BOSS ACTUALLY MEANS – AND HOW TO DO IT

How prepared are you for the realities of becoming your own boss? Use this quiz to test the viability of your business model and your vision for your new career.

1 *What does it actually mean to become your own boss?*
2 *What are all the necessary steps you will need to take in order to pre-empt and avoid any potential roadblocks to your business?*

3 How much of your initial budget should you spend on promotional materials? Which materials will best serve your business?
4 Will your hobby translate into a viable business model?
5 Will you be able to make enough money to sustain yourself by building a career around an erstwhile hobby?
6 How certain are you that there is a need for your offer in the marketplace?
7 How certain are you that other people will be as keen to pay for the output of your hobby as you are to do it?
8 How realistic are your expectations of profitability and sustainability in pursuing your hobby as your career?
9 If push comes to shove, would you rather keep your favourite pastime as a hobby which you will continue to enjoy to its maximum potential, or would you rather turn it into your new career even if that means accepting that you will no longer enjoy it nearly as much?
10 Is your vision for your new career realistic and workable?

Chapter 6 quiz

SETTING UP YOUR SOLO WORK LIFE

Where is the best place from which to work in your new career as your own boss? Use this quiz as a checklist to ensure you fully understand each of the options available to you, and to determine which one you think will work best for you.

1 Is working from home, renting an office or purchasing an office your best option?
2 Is it preferable to you to work alongside other likeminded people, albeit completely independent of them, or is it better to have your own secluded space?
3 Will the costs incurred in renting an office space (including the commute, parking etc.) be outweighed by the extra revenue you are able to generate?

4 Would a commute necessitated by renting an office space be a good or bad thing?
5 Will working in a dedicated work space help you to focus more effectively, boosting your productivity and profitability or can you work just as well peripatetically?
6 Will having other people around you during your working day help to motivate you or just provide unwanted distractions? (Bear in mind that they will not necessarily, or even likely, be involved in the same line or work as you.)
7 If you opt for renting a work space how long is the rental agreement? Can you opt out early without incurring a heavy penalty if you discover that it is not working for you?
8 Is purchasing an office space or other working environment a viable and financially sound option?
9 What are the merits of renting an office space on a very short-term contract?
10 Working from home might seem the obvious answer but what are some of the major drawbacks?

Chapter 7 quiz

EFFECTIVE HOME WORKING

How effective is your home working set-up? Use this quick test to highlight the changes you need to make to maximize the efficiency of your working environment.

1 Have you established a clear demarcation between your home life and your work life?
2 Have you ring-fenced both your time and your space?
3 Have you established home-working rules for yourself?
4 Have you established home-working rules for your family, and have they embraced them?
5 Have you created a workable synergy between your home and work life?
6 Would your home-working set-up pass muster in a large multinational?

7 *Does your office look and feel like a work space? Have you compromised this with the need to balance family life with work life?*

8 *Does entering your office automatically and effectively put you mentally straight into 'work mode'? If not, what is your budget for creating your ideal work space?*

9 *Have you established a routine for keeping your work space as neat, tidy and clean as the offices in a large multinational?*

10 *What improvements could you make to your home working set-up?*

Chapter 8 quiz

ACCENTUATING THE POSITIVES OF BEING YOUR OWN BOSS

What are the key advantages and disadvantages to becoming your own boss? How will you maximize the former whilst minimizing the latter? Use this quiz to test your knowledge in this area and highlight those things you need to implement in order to get the most from being your own boss.

1 *What are your key advantages over big corporate companies?*

2 *What are your key disadvantages versus big corporate companies?*

3 *How will you maximize the potential of each advantage whilst minimizing the drawbacks of each disadvantage?*

4 *What are the main advantages of making your own rules?*

5 *What are the main drawbacks of making your own rules?*

6 *Why is it important to find time for reflection in your working life?*

7 *What do you anticipate will be the biggest single boon to being your own boss?*

8 *What is your greatest fear about becoming your own boss?*

9 *How can you use downtime in your business to your advantage?*

10 *Why is taking regular breaks and even extended holidays crucial to the success of your business?*

Chapter 9 quiz

MAXIMIZING HOME–OFFICE POTENTIAL

Are you making the most of working from home? Equally importantly, are you avoiding the pitfalls? In what ways can you change your routine to maximize your home–office potential?

1 *What safeguards have you put in place to ensure that you get enough exercise to keep your mind working to its maximum potential?*
2 *Why is it especially important to 'commute' to work if you work from home?*
3 *As a home-alone worker, what are some of the biggest dangers to the efficiency of your business and how can you overcome them?*
4 *How can you avoid loneliness and isolation if you are a solo worker?*
5 *What are the disadvantages of flexibility in your working life?*
6 *Why might the security of your business be compromised?*
7 *How might you be compromising your clients' security?*
8 *What steps do you need to implement to safeguard sensitive data?*
9 *In what way is the phrase 'Lazy people take the most pains' commonly applicable to people who become their own boss?*
10 *Why is it important to 'spring clean' your hard drive on a regular basis?*

Chapter 10 quiz

TARGETS AND PLANNING

To realize your company's maximum potential it is vitally important to establish clear business targets and boundaries, and to provide yourself with the motivation to see you through the tough times to ensure you meet them. This checklist will help you highlight whether you have these in place, and whether they are sufficiently robust and realistic.

1 *What is your vision for your company? Do you have a defined roadmap with checkpoints at each major stage?*
2 *Are your targets falsely optimistic or pessimistic, or are they realistic?*
3 *How often will you review your targets?*
4 *Have you identified all the potential problems which might beset your business?*
5 *What are your problem-solving strategies to deal with them?*
6 *How will you plot your course to meeting your targets? How often will you review them?*
7 *What do your long- and short-term obituaries for yourself and your company look like?*
8 *To whom will you communicate your business plans to provide yourself with additional motivation?*
9 *What are the reasons you quit your job to become your own boss? Why is the grass actually greener on your side?*
10 *Why is it important to reward yourself for meeting your business objectives? How will you be rewarded?*

Chapter 11 quiz

MOBILE WORKING

How can you use the latest mobile communications technologies to give you and your business a competitive edge? Why does adoption of these technologies give you the freedom to be your own boss in just the way you want to be? Use this quiz to test your knowledge in this area and highlight those things you need to implement in order to get the most from being your own boss.

1 *How can you exploit mobile-working technologies to give you an increased level of workplace flexibility?*

2 *How can you capitalize on mobile working to build a better relationship with your clients, suppliers etc.?*

3 *How does mobile working create a freedom you can exploit in your working life?*

4 *What are your top three priorities for making the most of this freedom?*

5 *How will you use mobile technologies to shake up your working routine?*

6 *How will you ensure you are always ready to seize unexpected opportunities?*

7 *How can you turn downtime into a valuable opportunity to work?*

8 *How can you use mobile working to minimize costs?*

9 *How will you capitalize on your flexibility to create the perfect image of your company for your clients?*

10 *How can you use mobile working to streamline your working practices?*

Chapter 12 quiz

WORKING 5 TO 9

Would the opportunity to try out your business in the marketplace before taking the leap to making it your full-time occupation provide a much-needed test of its robustness? Or would this just be adding an extra, unnecessary hurdle? Would it be sensible to see if your business really can be profitable before giving up your day job or are you just looking for ways to delay committing yourself to it? Use this quiz to see if becoming a 5-to-9er is right for you.

1 *How passionate are you about your new business venture? Do you have the resolve to persevere when the going gets tough?*

2 *What is your vision for the business?*

3 *Do you see your business as a lucrative hobby or a business capable of supporting you financially?*

4 Do you hope to be able at some stage to concentrate on your business full time?

5 Are you prepared to put in the amount of work required, sacrificing most of your evenings and weekends?

6 Are you prepared to lose a good deal of your social life, as well as a good deal of sleep, to make your business successful?

7 What sort of support is offered for the 5-to-9er, and where is it available?

8 Do you need to test your offer in the marketplace before committing yourself to it full time?

9 Do you have a firm idea of the amount of work setting up a 5 to 9 enterprise is likely to entail?

10 Do you have enough working capital to give up your day job and does your business have the capacity to grow big enough, quickly enough to support you?

Chapter 13 quiz

IT FOR THE SOLO WORKER

What are the IT implications for your business? How can you leverage the opportunities they present to promote the growth of your business? What barriers to a successful business can be caused by not establishing a robust IT infrastructure or being unwilling to embrace it fully? Use this quiz to test your knowledge of the information technology available to your business and how to use it to best advantage.

1 Does information technology excite you or leave you cold? What is your current level of expertise in this area?

2 What is the greatest information resource ever created, and why is it at your constant disposal?

3 How can you utilize an effective communication infrastructure to ensure you never miss out on a single piece of work?

4 *How can the new-found freedom of being your own boss and the never-ending connectivity provided by modern IT cost you valuable business opportunities?*

5 *What are the pros and cons of each of the many connectivity tools at your disposal?*

6 *Which will provide a significant and tangible benefit to your business?*

7 *If you provide your business with only one piece of IT connectivity what should it be?*

8 *Do you have a sufficient quantity of relevant and interesting material to sustain a blog and/or Twitter stream for your business?*

9 *What are the cost implications of commissioning and maintaining viral games and/or apps for the iPhone, iPad, Ovi etc.?*

10 *Your clients have the right to expect you to have embraced at least the minimum of information technology tools. What are they?*

Chapter 14 quiz

ACCOUNTING FOR SUCCESSFUL BUSINESS

Do you understand the financial implications of running your own business? Do you have sufficient capital in place to begin trading? Use this quiz to ensure you have covered all the bases for getting and keeping your finances in order.

1 *When should you begin the process of getting your new company's finances set up?*

2 *When is the best time to open a business bank account for your company?*

3 *How much initial capital will you need to have in place to start your company, and how much as a contingency fund?*

4 *Which trading medium will be best for your business – sole trader, limited company or partnership?*

5   *Will it be advisable to employ the services of an accountant?*
6   *Which receipts do you need to keep and how should they be filed?*
7   *How much money should you keep readily accessible to cope with any unforeseen circumstances?*
8   *What sort of insurances do you need to have in place to cover you and your business in case of emergencies?*
9   *Is there any funding available to your business?*
10 *What are the pros and cons of registering your company for purchase tax?*

Chapter 15 quiz

DEALING WITH CLIENTS

Are you prepared for the complex politics of dealing with clients? Do you know how best to foster good long-term relationships with them, to generate future work easily and even to get paid early? Use this quick quiz to test your knowledge.

1   *When should you slow down your recruitment drive for new business?*
2   *What are the twin pillars of supplier/client relationships?*
3   *When should you realign your offer to match your clients' needs?*
4   *How can you make yourself and your company an indispensable part of your clients' business machine.*
5   *How can you try to ensure that you get paid on time, or even early?*
6   *Why is it important to have all agreed costs and a timescale for payment in full and* in writing *before beginning a project?*
7   *What is the earliest point at which it is acceptable to submit an invoice?*
8   *Why is it important to establish a good one-to-one relationship with someone in the accounts department?*

9 *How do you know when it is time to let go of a client, and how can this be achieved in such a way as to leave the door open for future work?*

10 *Are your prices and terms of business fair and competitive? Do you keep track of the market to ensure that they always remain so? When is it reasonable to fight your corner over your prices and timescale for payment and how should you go about doing so?*

Index